Discovering The Lleyn Peninsula and Anglesey

ACKNOWLEDGEMENTS

Selecting all the photographs and the research for Discovering The Lleyn Peninsula and Anglesey has given me a great deal of contentment, nevertheless, without contributions from many individuals, the complete work in its entirety would not have been possible. I would like to thank everybody that has contributed towards the book and would particularly like to extend my appreciation at the outset to HRH Prince Philip for taking the time to peruse the photographs and to reflect on what is a most beautiful and scenic part of the British Isles.

My grateful thanks extend to Andrew Thomas at the Ffestiniog & Welsh Highland Railway, for his generous help, to ensure accuracy of information on the oldest railway company in the world still running trains, and for the kind permission for the use of the photographs. For the consent to use the images of Portmeirion I would like to acknowledge the help from Meurig Jones the estate manager. For consent to use the interior photographs, of what can only be described as some of Wales most beautiful of churches, I would like to express thanks to the Reverend Nick Hawkins, Llangwnadl, Reverend Susie Williams, Pystill and Reverend Madelaine Brady of St. Cwyfan's Church Anglesey. My appreciation goes to Flight Sqn Ldr John M McFall, Flight Sergeant Andy Carnall at RAF Valley and Barbara Hiddleston Engagement and Communications Officer Royal Air Force Valley for their generous help and assistance to ensure the accuracy of the section covering the station at Valley. Recognition goes out to the RNLI at Moelfre, in particular Rod Pace, Coxswain Anthony Barclay and specifically crew member and Paramedic Dave Massey for his generosity in taking time out, detailing the stations past history and present day rescues. Dave also provided images of the lifeboat in action, and gave kind permission to use them within the book. The RNLI station is well worth a visit, and you can be assured of a warm welcome. One of the unseen tasks of publishing is that of proof reading and without this vital function the whole work can be undone, with this in mind I would like to acknowledge the extremely generous involvement from Julie Pack who has also facilitated my earlier publications

As with my previous books, special recognition is extended to Tina who has spent immeasurable hours in what can only be described as one of the most scenic parts of Britain, striving to capture the perfect shot and has again contributed to a good deal of the photographs within the book. To Nick again for his contributions and helping with the equipment. Last but not least I would like to acknowledge DB Publishing for their enthusiasm and in particular Laura Smith and Steve Caron for publishing Discovering The Lleyn Peninsula and Anglesey.

First published in Great Britain in 2012 by The Derby Books Publishing Company Limited, 3 The Parker Centre, Derby, DE21 4SZ.

ISBN 978-1-78091-001-7
Printed and bound by Melita Press, Malta.

Discovering
The Lleyn Peninsula
and Anglesey

John Bailey

Photography by John and Tina Bailey
Foreword by HRH The Duke of Edinburgh Prince Philip

DB PUBLISHING

The golden sands of Nefyn provide a most spectacular view east to the lofty peak of Yr Eifl standing 1,849ft above sea level, the true summit of Llŷn.

CONTENTS

FOREWORD

I suppose one should never be surprised by a service appointment, but I was totally mystified when I was appointed to HMS 'Glendower', at a place with the unpronounceable name of Pwllheli in North Wales. I had only recently returned from the far East at the end of the war against Japan, and this was my introduction to the peace-time Navy in spring 1946. When I got to the railway ticket office, I had to spell out my destination, as I had no idea how to pronounce it.

When I eventually reached HMS 'Glendower', it turned out to be a Butlin's holiday camp, built just before the war, that had been taken over by the Navy as a New Entry Training Establishment. What very soon became apparent to me was the place was situated in the most glorious countryside, and I thoroughly enjoyed my time there.

When the author of this book sent me a proof copy, his remarkable photographs brought back many happy memories. I hope that looking at the pictures may persuade you to have a look at the real thing some day.

HRH The Duke of Edinburgh Prince Philip

INTRODUCTION

I have to confess a deep underlying affection of The Lleyn Peninsula having spent seven long summers here in the late seventies through to the early eighties.

The Llŷn, the arm in the Irish Sea, extends some 30 miles west from Snowdonia in North West Wales. An extraordinary landscape of beautiful fishing villages and historic towns, where ancient tracks are still to be found, the landscape enhanced by numerous white-washed farms and a patchwork of enclosed fields. No more than 8 miles wide giving easy access to the contrasting north and south coasts, it was designated an area of outstanding natural beauty in 1956. Iron Age hill forts, Neolithic tombs and standing stones are all to be found and due to the remoteness of the area it has remained unspoilt. The peninsula benefits from the Gulf Stream, creating a micro climate on its southern shores bringing warmer weather and higher sea temperatures than would be expected at this latitude and relatively little rainfall compared to the lofty regions of Snowdonia. The back bone of the peninsula is dominated by the 1,849ft Yr Eifl where on a clear day the majestic sweep of Cardigan Bay can be seen as far south as St David's Head in Pembrokeshire.

The Welsh name for this area is Pen Llŷn. The spelling of Llŷn on ordnance survey maps is 'Lleyn' which is said to be more correct for English but locally Llŷn is used, although other variations are sometimes found. Welsh is a very descriptive language and the spelling of place names can vary so I have used the latest ordnance survey maps as a point of reference.

Castles at Criccieth and Caernarfon are a reminder of the areas important historical past. Criccieth Castle was built during the 13th century for Llywelyn the Great. Captured by Edward I in 1283, Criccieth Castle was subsequently destroyed in 1404 after it was besieged by Owain Glyndwr. Caernarfon Castle was completed in 1330 with work having begun in 1283 by Edward I and remains today one of the best preserved castles in Britain.

The Llŷn is blessed with beautiful churches, most within sight of the sea, providing shelter for pilgrims en route to Bardsey Island. Tradition has it that 20,000 saints are buried on the island. The great little trains of Wales have a foot hold in the peninsula with the Ffestiniog Railway and Welsh Highland Railway terminus at Porthmadog. Originally founded in 1832 by an act of Parliament the Ffestiniog Railway was built to transport slate from the quarries above Blaenau Ffestiniog and as the slate industry succeeded so did the railway until its closure in 1946. The line was thankfully reopened in 1956 by a new band of railway enthusiasts. The Ffestiniog Railway is now a major tourist attraction in Wales and has led the way for many other preserved railway lines that would have been lost forever. The Welsh Highland Railway now connects Caernarfon in the north to Porthmadog. The town of Porthmadog takes its name from William Madocks who in the early 19th century created the town and built the Cob, a mile long embankment across the mouth of the Afon Glaslyn, reclaiming 7,000 acres of land.

The southern coast is home to the main resorts of Criccieth and Pwllheli with the charming fishing villages of Llanbedrog, Abersoch, and Aberdaron. On the more rugged north coast nestles the small coves of Porth Oer, Porth Iago, Porth Colmon and the larger Porth Dinllaen. Porth Dinllaen was once an important shipping centre with plans to become the main port for Ireland before the decision was made by the House of Commons in 1837 to opt for Holyhead. Today it remains a pleasant fishing village.

The Llŷn can be summed up by a Welsh poem that says Llŷn is a place where spirits find peace.

Connected to the mainland by the splendour of Thomas Telford's suspension bridge opened in 1823, as a result of the act of union, is the Isle of Anglesey Sir Ynys Mon. Anglesey has over 100 miles of diverse coastal environment ranging from sea cliffs, salt marshes, dunes and mud flats all providing a spectacular habitat for a variety of birds, plants and wildlife. Edward I's iron ring was completed with the building of a castle at Beaumaris overlooking the Menai Strait and the mountains of Snowdonia with Beaumaris today a main yachting centre. The village of Newborough in the south was created when the population of Llanfaes were relocated to make way for the building of the castle. Anglesey boasts the village with the longest official place name in the British Isles, Llanfairpwllgwyngyllgogerychwyndrobwllllantysiliogogogoch.

Being an island off the north west coast of Wales, can bring windy conditions at times when south westerly gales blow and this power was harnessed in the 18th and 19th century, with over 50 windmills said to have been in existence. Most are now in a state of disrepair or have disappeared altogether, but thankfully some have been preserved, with Llynnon Mill the only working windmill in Wales and now an agricultural museum. Anglesey is blessed with mile upon mile of golden sands with magnificent beaches on the west coast at Aberffraw and Llanddwyn with Traeth-Coch or Red Wharf Bay on the east coast. It is the magnificent landscape and a rich history that will live long in your memory should you visit, and will keep alive a desire to return one day.

John Bailey

PORTHMADOG AND THE FFESTINIOG RAILWAY

The river or Afon Glaslyn begins its journey to the sea 2,000ft above sea level in a cwm on the eastern flanks of Snowdon. From the cwm the river runs east to Llyn Llydaw then flows through majestic mountain scenery turning south west to continue its journey through Nantgwynant and onto Beddgelert. The journey then continues south through the Aberglaslyn Pass ahead of reaching the sea at Porthmadog, a distance of some 14 miles from its source above Llyn Llydaw.

Porthmadog and Tremadog developed out of William Madocks desire to reclaim the wide Glaslyn estuary and 7,000 acres of land by building a mile long embankment known as the Cob between 1808 and 1811. A harbour was built between 1821 and 1825 to enable the transportation of the slate from the quarries above Blaenau Ffestiniog. Porthmadog took its name from Madocks, as translated its meaning is Madog's Port. Madocks was born in 1773, a member of a wealthy London family with firm links to North Wales. His plans also included establishing Porthmadog and the Cob as an integral part of the rail link from London to Dublin with a port on the north Llŷn coast at Porth Dinllaen, destined to be the departure point for Ireland. It was an ambitious plan that left the family close to bankruptcy when it was announced that Holyhead was chosen as the preferred route.

The port would, however, in due course bring substantial prosperity to the area with estimates of over 115,000 tons of Blaenau slate leaving by sea annually during the peak in the late 1800s. Rich in maritime history, Porthmadog today is a bustling town and the gateway to the Lleyn Peninsula, the home of the Ffestiniog Railway.

Porthmadog and nearby Borth-y-Gest grew to become an important shipbuilding area with over 260 vessels constructed between 1825 and 1913. The end of shipbuilding came when the last vessel built in 1913, the Gestiana, sunk on her maiden voyage.

William Madocks reclaimed the wide Glaslyn estuary and 7,000 acres of land by building the mile long embankment, known as the Cob, between 1808 and 1811.

Harbour station Porthmadog marks the gateway to the Lleyn Peninsula set at the northern end of the Cob.

The *Earl* at the starting point of the 12 miles of ascent to Blaenau Ffestiniog. The initial section of the line has to cross the mile long embankment known as the Cob.

Rheilffordd Ffestiniog was originally founded in 1832 by an act of Parliament as a gravity and horse drawn line to transport slate from the quarries above Blaenau Ffestiniog. As the slate industry developed so did the railway, along with Porthmadog. Some confusion has at times surrounded the correct spelling of Ffestiniog with the adage, one F for the railway two for the town, being frequently used during the late 1970s. The act of Parliament incorporated the railway as the Festiniog Railway Company. Throughout its development it was always known locally as the Ffestiniog Railway, predictably giving its links with the town. Today the double Ff is used on all railway literature, keeping its close association with Blaenau Ffestiniog; however, the coat of arms still reflects its legal entity.

The railway was to enjoy a successful period when output from the quarries grew along with increasing passenger numbers. This success attracted engineers from several continents to see how the railway had introduced ground-breaking engineering solutions that would, in due course, influence the construction of many railways throughout the world.

The first steam traction was introduced on the 23.5 inch track in July 1863. In 1869 an act was passed to increase to double track but it proved too costly so an ingenious solution was found by the engineer Robert Fairlie who designed a more powerful locomotive that could negotiate tight curves and steep gradients. He created an engine with double bogies with one long central firebox and driving position looking like back-to-back engines known as a Double Fairlie.

The decline in the demand for slate and other means of transportation would instigate closure of the line in 1946. Pioneering railway enthusiasts at the time were determined to reopen the line and thankfully their ambitions were realised 10 years later.

1958 saw the line restored as far as Tan-y-Bwlch but the ultimate aim was to reach Blaenau Ffestiniog. A tremendous amount of work would be necessary to achieve that aim as it required a deviation from the original route, now flooded due to the Hydro electric scheme near Tanygrisiau. Work would necessitate building a loop at Dduallt to raise the height of the line and a new tunnel had to be constructed at Moelwyn.

1982 saw the final goal to run trains from Porthmadog through to Blaenau Ffestiniog being achieved 150 years on from the first act of Parliament.

The line side equipment is well greased to withstand the regular battering from the salt water spray when storms sweep in from the west.

The Ffestiniog railway's works are located at Boston lodge at the southern end of the Cob, built on the site of the quarry used to provide the building material for the construction of the mile long embankment between 1808 and 1811.

The locomotive *Earl of Merioneth* was the first new locomotive to be constructed at Boston Lodge since closure of the line in 1946. Work began in 1972 with completion seeing her enter passenger service in 1979. The *Earl* was built to replace *Livingston Thompson*, which is now on permanent display at the National Railway Museum, York. The original locomotive *Livingston Thompson* built in 1886 was renamed *Taliesin* in 1932, the last Double Fairlie built by the old Ffestiniog Railway Company. Another name change was brought about in the early 1960s as it was suggested that His Royal Highness the Duke of Edinburgh would be delighted to have his name on a Ffestiniog Railway locomotive. So in 1961 the locomotive was renamed *Earl of Merioneth* one of the titles held by HRH Prince Phillip, Duke of Edinburgh. The locomotive is a Double Fairlie but built to a modern style, unlike the railways two other Double Fairlie's *Merddin Emrys* and *David Lloyd George*. The *Earl* has now been converted to burn coal rather than oil, brought about by the difference in the price between fuels.

The lamp positioned at the front of the locomotive.

Opposite: An ex-Lynton and Barnstable carriage provides very comfortable third class accommodation.

First class travel is available on the Ffestiniog Railway.

Opposite: The track crossing the mile long embankment.

One F for the railway two for the town. The *Earl's* green livery presents a prominent background for the Festiniog Railway coat of arms.

The drivers eye view from the cab of *Earl of Merioneth*.

Equipment well greased to withstand the forces of nature.

The brass nameplate on the locomotive *Earl of Merioneth* the first new locomotive to be constructed at Boston Lodge since closure of the line in 1946.

The *Earl of Merioneth* hauls the first passenger service of the day out of Porthmadog. The Earl seen here in bright sunshine with leaden skies forming a contrasting backdrop highlighting smoke and steam as The Earl embarks on the scenic 12 miles journey to the station at Blaenau Ffestiniog over 700ft above sea level.

A close look at the *Earl's* driving mechanism.

Cnicht and the Moelwyns sport their winter coats providing a most dramatic backdrop with the cool winter air highlighting a trail of steam at the beginning of the journey to Blaenau Ffestiniog.

THE WELSH HIGHLAND RAILWAY

The original line, opened in 1923 was an amalgamation of several separate railways which closed in 1936, mainly as a result of the decline of the slate industry. The track was lifted in 1941 as part of the war effort and the trackbed gradually returned to nature.

By the end of the 1960s, the first tentative efforts were underway to restore the line, beginning with the first short section opened to passenger traffic on the former standard gauge trackbed at Pen y Mount in 1980.

With the Ffestiniog route completed back to Blaenau Ffestiniog in the late 1980s, thoughts turned to creating a new rail link from Caernarfon to Porthmadog and creating a 40 mile railway between Caernarfon and Blaenau Ffestiniog. 1997 saw the first trains run the three miles from Caernarfon to Dinas, along the course of the old Bangor to Afon Wen line, closed as part of the Beeching cuts in the 1960s.

By 2003, with the help of funding from the Millennium Commission, the European Regional Development Fund and the Welsh Development Agency, track had reached the halfway point at Rhyd Ddu at the foot of Snowdon, with the section opened by HRH Prince Charles on 18 August that year. Further funding from the Welsh Assembly and the EU was secured in 2004 to enable the final 12 miles to Porthmadog to be rebuilt. Together with a hugely successful public appeal, the total rebuilding cost of £28 million was reached with the final section of track being laid into Porthmadog Harbour Station in 2009.

The completed railway was opened on 20 April 2011 – 175 years to the day from the opening of the Ffestiniog Railway in 1836.

The Welsh Highland Railway starts a spectacular 25 mile scenic journey from beneath the castle walls at Caernarfon. The trains – hauled by the world's most powerful narrow gauge steam locomotives – climb from sea level to over 650ft on the foothills of Snowdon, before zigzagging dramatically down the steep hillside to reach Beddgelert, nestling in the heart of the National Park, then continuing through the magnificent Aberglaslyn Pass and on to Porthmadog.

NG/Gl6 Beyer-Garrett No 143 providing steam power for the Welsh Highland Railway was originally built for work in South Africa. Seen here returning to Harbour Station after its first test run on the WHR.

Opposite: The first public service train on the Welsh Highland from Porthmadog. Single Fairlie *Taliesin* runs round at Hafod y Llyn on Saturday 8 January 2011.

Work began in 2006 to complete the project with volunteer tracklayers reaching their destination in Porthmadog in 2009. This entailed replacing missing bridges and a 'flat crossing' of the Cambrian Coast main line and a tramway section through the streets of Porthmadog. The railway's original fleet of two NG/G16 Beyer Garratts Nos. 138 & 143 were added to with the delivery of NG/G16 No. 87, rebuilt at the Ffestiniog Railway's Boston Lodge Works after a private donation of £500,000 was received to cover the costs of purchase and restoration.

New carriages have also been built at Boston Lodge for use on the Welsh Highland Railway increasing the level of passenger comfort offered. A new Observation Pullman Carriage entered service in 2009 and was named *Glaslyn* by Her Majesty the Queen during a visit to the railway in early 2010.

PORTMEIRION

The wooded peninsula across the estuary at the southern end of the Cob is the home of the Italianate village of Portmeirion. Although not strictly on the Lleyn Peninsula it is worthy of a visit being so close and easily accessed by road from Minffordd two miles south east of Porthmadog, before beginning our journey west along the Lleyn Peninsula.

An alternative option on foot begins from the station at Porthmadog. A path runs across the top of the cob following the Ffestiniog Railway before reaching the railway works at Boston Lodge. Drop down onto the A487 for a short distance before taking a path on your right. The path rises up the wooded peninsula eventually emerging at the car park above Portmeirion. A fee is charged for entrance to the village.

Gerald of Wales first made reference to Portmeirion in 1188. 'We crossed the Traeth Mawr and the Traeth Bychan. These are two arms of the sea, one large and one small. Two stone castles have been built there recently. The one called Castell Deudraeth belongs to the sons of Cynan and is situated in the Eifionydd area, facing the northern Mountains'.

In 1925 Sir William Clough acquired what was known as Aber la changing the name to Portmeirion, using the connection of port as on the coast and Meirion from the county name Merioneth. He wrote in his book *Portmeirion, The Place and its Meaning* originally published in 1963, 'Some day, somewhere, I would even assuredly erect a whole group of buildings on my own chosen site for my own satisfaction; an ensemble that would body forth my chafing ideas of fitness and gaiety and indeed be me'.

The building of the Italianate village was completed in two stages, 1925–39 saw the major buildings erected while the period between 1954–76 was known for its Palladian style infilling, salvaging several buildings from demolition sites.

Portmeirion was used as the setting for the 1960s television series *The Prisoner* that went on to achieve cult status starring Patrick McGoohan. The series ran for 17 episodes and introduced many famous actors including Leo McKern, Peter Bowles, Eric Portman, Patrick Cargill, Paul Eddington and Donald Sinden.

The Panethon or Dome at Portmeirion.

Portmeirion from Gwyllt woods.

Opposite: Portmeirion from the gazebo shrouded in mellifluous autumn light looking across Traeth Bach to Ynys Gifftan.

Nestled on the shores of the Afon Glaslyn, Borth-y-Gest provides sheltered moorings for numerous small boats, with the mountains of North Wales dominating distant views.

BORTH-Y-GEST

Borth-y-Gest is easily reached from Porthmadog, a short walk beginning at the bridge at the harbour following the quayside. Continue on behind the yacht club, past boatyards, over the hill to drop down into Borth. This is the beginning of the Lleyn Peninsula coastal path that continues west from Borth to the sandy expanses of Black Rock sands at Morfa Bychan, while providing spectacular views across the bay to the Irish Sea. Across the bay from the jetty the view looking east encompasses the Cob at Porthmadog, whereas the view south is dominated by the distant Rhinogs rising above 2,300ft, providing an impressive backdrop for Harlech Castle set on a rocky crag. The building of Harlech Castle was begun by Edward I in 1283 as part of his fortification of North Wales.

The Victorian seaside village of Borth-y-Gest has maintained a charming quaintness that has remained relatively untouched by modern day commercialisation, set in a natural bowl and surrounded by deciduous woodlands with many fine examples of ancient Welsh oak. Nestled on the shores of the Afon Glaslyn, Borth-y-Gest provides sheltered moorings for numerous small boats with the backdrop of the terraces of Victorian houses running down to the sea shore. Older than its close neighbour, two centuries ago Borth-y-Gest would have been the regular haunt of smugglers. Few communities would have been disadvantaged by the work of William Madock's building of the Cob at Porthmadog but here at Borth-y-Gest that was the case. It was here that the perilous journey across the sands of Traeth Mawr to Harlech began. Locals would have received a precious income from guiding strangers across the wide expanse of Tremadog Bay.

The sands of the estuary are a paradise for birdwatchers, home to many species including oystercatchers, redshank and curlew.

A quintessential coastal scene.

Opposite: The deciduous woodlands provide a serene backdrop to Borth-y-Gest while the sands of the estuary are home to many species of birds including oystercatchers, redshank and curlew.

The two mile expanse of sands at Black Rock are backed by sand dunes and towered over by the mass of Moel-y-Gest, the wind creating mini sand storms on a blustery day.

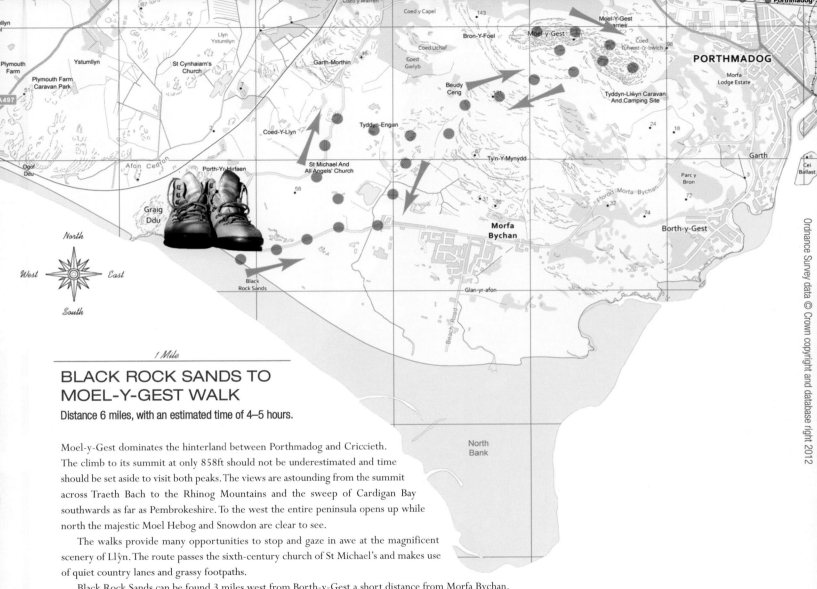

Ordnance Survey data © Crown copyright and database right 2012

1 Mile

BLACK ROCK SANDS TO MOEL-Y-GEST WALK

Distance 6 miles, with an estimated time of 4–5 hours.

Moel-y-Gest dominates the hinterland between Porthmadog and Criccieth. The climb to its summit at only 858ft should not be underestimated and time should be set aside to visit both peaks. The views are astounding from the summit across Traeth Bach to the Rhinog Mountains and the sweep of Cardigan Bay southwards as far as Pembrokeshire. To the west the entire peninsula opens up while north the majestic Moel Hebog and Snowdon are clear to see.

The walks provide many opportunities to stop and gaze in awe at the magnificent scenery of Llŷn. The route passes the sixth-century church of St Michael's and makes use of quiet country lanes and grassy footpaths.

Black Rock Sands can be found 3 miles west from Borth-y-Gest a short distance from Morfa Bychan.

An alternative route to Black Rock Sands is to be found off the main A497 taking the unclassified road on your left if heading from Porthmadog at Wern almost immediately before the railway bridge.

Follow this minor road for 2 miles where parking is available at Black Rock Sands car park on the beach or on the roadside if space permits at grid reference 531 373.

The beautiful setting for the church of St Michael's is enhanced with the awe inspiring views across Tremadog Bay to Traeth Bach and Harlech Castle.

The walk to the summit of Moel-y-Gest begins heading north; once you can pull yourself away from the spectacular two mile stretch of beach. The foreshore is backed by sand dunes with many caves to be found at the headland in the shadow of Black Rock.

Take the road bearing in the direction of Morfa Bychan for a short distance before following the track on your left where the road begins to bear right.

Keep to this track through the caravan and camping site to access a track leading up past a cottage and then immediately pass through a gate on your left before reaching the second dwelling. Once into the field head for the gap in the stone wall on your right where the path ascends the hillside to emerge at the kissing gate at the top corner of the field leading to the tiny Church. Pass through another kissing gate to enter the churchyard of St Michael's Treflys, built during the sixth century.

Continue through the churchyard to access the road all the while taking time to admire the delightful little church in its peaceful location with beautiful views across the bay from its elevated position and north-west to the summit of Moel-y-Gest.

Once on the lane turn right heading downhill through a series of twists and turns before taking a track on your right, easily identified from the two white stone pillars, that will eventually bring you to farm buildings. Continue ahead between the cottages and out buildings through two gates across a grassy path and a small stream, to emerge at another set of farm buildings at Tyddyn-adi. Continue through the farmyard taking the gate on your left just before the track that descends back to Morfa Bychan.

The route passes farm buildings ahead of reaching Tyddyn-adi farm below the western summit of Moel-y-Gest.

Head across a grassy path, cross a small stream to emerge at Tyddyn-adi farm. The summit of Moel-y-Gest dominates the distant views.

Cross the field to a gap in the wall fording a small stream heading upward until reaching the stone wall. Turn left to follow the grass path in the direction of some trees, disregarding the inviting entrance on your right to take the path that seemingly descends away to your left. In a short while follow the path that ascends to cross a wall, then head diagonally across a rise before reaching another stone wall. In the right corner there is a stone ladder. Once crossed, head in the direction of the base of the hill crossing another stone wall until reaching the base for the final ascent of Moel-y-Gest. No direct route is clear and some scrambling is required to reach the summit trig point 858ft above sea level.

The serene character of the lower slopes of Moel-y-Gest is enhanced during spring when new lambs abound.

This standing stone, part of a wall is close to the final ascent of the western summit.

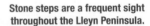

Stone steps are a frequent sight throughout the Lleyn Peninsula.

An unexcavated hill fort is located on the western peak.

34

Once atop, if the weather is kind the views are remarkable with Moel Hebog away to the north 2,560ft above sea level and beyond the Snowdon range, Yr Wyddfa standing proud 3,561ft above sea level. Sit on the exposed rocks to the south of the trig point below the summits highest peak where in a while you will be rewarded with buzzards circling not overhead but beneath the summit watching all the while as they glide on the currents of air before swooping to catch their prey. An unexcavated hill fort is located on the western peak.

The two summits, western and eastern, are connected by a ridge that offers spectacular views of the coast and mountains. To the south the views are awesome across Traeth Bach to Harlech and the mountains inland with the entire sweep of Cardigan Bay visible as far south as Pembrokeshire. To the north the lofty peaks of Moel Hebog and Snowdon summit 'Yr Wyddfa' are easily identifiable but spend a while to identify the other lofty heights of Snowdonia. Once rested continue along the ridge to reach the eastern summit at 793ft above sea level, though easier options are available using some of the lower paths. The views from the eastern summit are equally as awe inspiring as its western companion as you are now set high above Porthmadog, with the mile long embankment of the Cob helping to highlight the vastness of the reclaimed Glaslyn Estuary. If timing is right and, with a good pair of binoculars, you can sit and admire the spectacle of a Ffestiniog Railway engine steaming from the station below on its outward journey the length of the Cob to Minffordd then fading into the hillside on its way to Blaenau Ffestiniog.

To the north are the lofty peaks of Moel Hebog and Snowdon summit 'Yr Wyddfa'.

The triangulation pillar is positioned just below the western summit.

The return part of the walk is begun initially heading back towards the trig point to a rocky outcrop where a path becomes visible leading down to the wall at the foot of the main hill. The route back to Black Rock follows the outward journey to the farm at Tyddyn-adi.

The view from the eastern summit provides a bird's-eye view of Porthmadog, the cob and the reclaimed Glaslyn Estuary with the Rhinog and Cadair Idris mountain ranges breathtakingly visible on a clear day.

The ridge can be crossed to reach the eastern summit with views afforded back to the trig point on the higher western peak.

Looking west from the eastern summit. A ridge connects the two summits although easier options are available using some of the lower level paths.

The remains of a Neolithic stone-built burial chamber, Cist Cerrig.

A short distance before reaching the farm you will almost certainly glimpse to the west as you descend the hillside, Cist Cerrig, three upright stones, the remains of a Neolithic stone-built burial chamber, although the covering cairn no longer remains. Once back at the farm, take the track on your left to continue in the direction of Morfa Bychan passing another caravan and camping site to gain the minor road from Porthmadog. Turn right to follow the road back to the car park at Black Rock Sands.

To the west of the two mile stretch of sand our next destination can be seen. Criccieth Castle sits proudly high above the town on its rocky promontory. The quiet lane from Black Rock Sands passes the church of St Michael's before dropping down between trees and hedgerows that are awash with the delicate white flowers of wood anemones during early spring.

Wood anemone abounds during spring their leaves remaining well into summer. The plant takes its name from the Greek word for wind, anemos, as the slender flowers shake in the wind.

Unlike the castles of Harlech and Caernarfon, Beaumaris and Conwy, Criccieth was built by the Welsh Prince Llywelyn ap Iorwerth (Llywelyn the Great) between 1230 and 1240.

41

CRICCIETH CASTLE

As we approach Criccieth the castle dominates the hinterland, standing proud above the town with a commanding view of the whole sweep of Tremadog Bay. The original castle, a much smaller structure, was used as a fortress and a prison. Unlike the castles of Harlech and Caernarfon, Beaumaris and Conwy, Criccieth was built by the Welsh Prince Llywelyn ap Iorwerth (Llywelyn the Great) between 1230 and 1240. Gwynedd was always the stronghold of the princes and Llywelyn set about castle building here at Criccieth, Dolbadarn above Llyn Padarn and Dolwyddelan, close to Conwy. Some 30 years after it was built Llywelyn's grandson Llywelyn ap Gruffydd (Llywelyn the Last) enlarged the castle with the structure covering most of the hilltop with an addition of two new towers.

Criccieth Castle was taken over by Edward I in 1283 after he set about fortifying the rebellious lands of North Wales in 1277. The English King's victory over the Welsh was subsequently celebrated at Nefyn in 1284 with a jousting tournament.

The north was always a strong hold of the Welsh with invaders supplies easily cut off en route through the mountain terrain by the enemy. Edward I saw the building of a series of castles on the coast as the answer, as they could easily be supplied by sea. 1283 saw building begin on the major castles of Caernarfon, Harlech and Conwy.

Following his successful campaign against the Welsh the King set about extending and fortifying Criccieth Castle with the works completed by 1290. This was to have been a wise move as the Welsh rebels attempted to siege the castle in 1292 under the leadership of Madog ap Llywelyn, a relative of Llywelyn the Great. Edward I's plan had worked for the position of the castle was a prominent fact in it being unconquerable with reinforcement coming by sea from Ireland.

Criccieth Castle was taken over by Edward I in 1283, having set about fortifying the rebellious lands of North Wales in 1277.

The castle was to suffer a long period of neglect, apart from some repairs carried out by the late Lord Harlech. Things were to change for the good of the castle in 1923 when it was placed in the hands of the Ministry of Works. Over a six year period repairs were carried out to ensure that the castle structure would remain in its present condition.

Unfortunately, little remains of the guardrooms on the lower level.

Opposite: The castle's twin towered gatehouse overlooks the town.

Opposite: The view east from the castle walls takes in the sweep of Tremadog Bay to Black Rock Sands with the modest heights of Moel-y-Gest taking centre stage. The distant peaks of Snowdonia shrouded in summer cloud.

The outlook from the castle instils a sense of its strategic position high above Tremadog Bay, the uninterrupted view inland and the steep cliffs of the rocky promontory provided protection against invasion by sea.

The massive gatehouse dominates the hilltop with the towers protected by arrow slits and battlements. The gatehouse passage would have been complete with portcullis, and murder holes would have opened down onto the passage, allowing liquids and missiles to be used on any advancing enemy.

All that remains of the inner rooms of the gatehouse are the lower guardrooms and part of what would have been residential quarters on the upper floors. The inner ward is somewhat smaller than the external view of the towers would suggest.

Llywelyn the Great had built the castle in a diamond shape almost certainly fashioned by the contours of the hilltop. The stone curtain walling on the seaward flank suggested that Llywelyn had little fear of invasion from that direction given that the hillside drops steeply down to the coast.

After his capture of the castle in 1823, Edward I undertook a programme of extensive renovation including heightening the gatehouse towers, adding a new tower and strengthening the Engine Tower located on the northern end. The Engine Tower would have housed the catapult or siege engine which heightened the effect of mediaeval warfare. The tower also housed latrine shafts in the east wall, an indication that the structure originally had two upper floors.

The view across Cardigan Bay encompasses Harlech and the distant Rhinog's.

The plaque details the function of the engine tower.

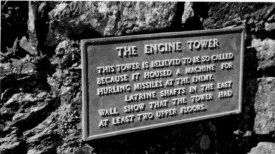

THE ENGINE TOWER
THIS TOWER IS BELIEVED TO BE SO CALLED BECAUSE IT HOUSED A MACHINE FOR HURLING MISSILES AT THE ENEMY. LATRINE SHAFTS IN THE EAST WALL SHOW THAT THE TOWER HAD AT LEAST TWO UPPER FLOORS.

All that remains of the inner rooms of the gatehouse are the lower guardrooms and part of what would have been residential quarters on the upper floors.

The entire stretch of the southern coast of the peninsula is visible from the western end of the castle with the distant peak of Carn Fadryn prominent on the skyline.

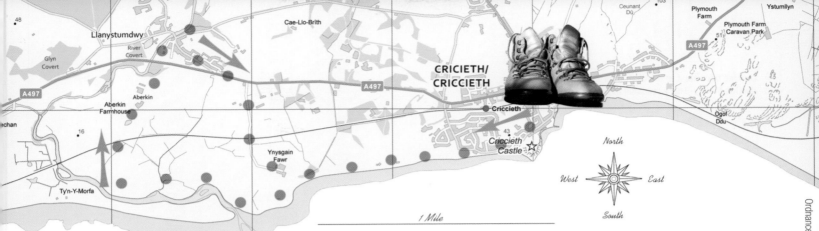

Criccieth developed from the early 1800s when a turnpike road ran through from Tremadog as part of the great plan of William Madocks to establish a main port to Ireland at Porth Dinllaen on the north coast. Perhaps more significantly, it was the coming of the railways in 1828 that elevated Criccieth to a popular seaside destination with the early Victorian holiday makers. Today it is still a popular seaside resort with shallow, crystal clear waters that lap the golden sands and pebbles warmed by the influence of the Gulf Stream, helping to create a micro climate while the curving arm of Llŷn protects the southern coast from the worst of the prevailing winds.

CRICCIETH TO LLANYSTUMDWY WALK

Distance 5.5 miles, with an estimated time of 3 hours.

A very undemanding walk over the flat coastal area to the west of Criccieth, continuing inland along the banks of the Afon Dwyfor to the home and last resting place of Lloyd George, the delightful village of Llanystumdwy. Time can be spent in Llanystumdwy with a pub and cafe providing refreshment while a visit to a memorial and museum dedicated to the former Prime Minister provides a fascinating insight to the great Welsh statesman's life.

Begin from the esplanade at grid reference 500 378. Walk past the castle to the shore continuing west along the seafront until the road turns inland. Continue along the shore passing through a kissing gate keeping the sea on your left along a path sheltered from the sea breeze by the dense growth of gorse. Pass a delightfully situated cottage, then continue behind a derelict cottage to follow the boundary to take the left path back to the cliff top, where you will soon to be rewarded with distant views south east across Tremadog bay to the Harlech and the Rhinog's beyond. Inland the views unfold to reveal the highest point on Llŷn, Yr Eifl. The path now drops down to the shoreline where you continue, ignoring the track on your right, to follow the coast until reaching the estuary of the Afon Dwyfor, where the pathway needs no explanation, following the banks of the river. Pass on, ignoring a track on your right. Easy walking is now provided with the wooden platforms taking you across the boggy ground.

Sunlight and stormy skies create a striking contrast.

Looking back west to Criccieth from the the Afon Dwyfor, Moel-y-Gest dominates the backdrop.

At the mouth of the Afon Dwyfor the route begins to veer inland. The Afon Dwyfor rises high up in Cwm Dwyfor under the shadow of Mynydd Tal-y-mignedd over 2,000ft above sea level deep into Snowdonia close to Beddgelert Forest.

In just under half a mile you come across a stile on your right, take this to cross a meadow and railway line (take extreme care as this is the main Barmouth to Pwllheli line) to reach a track that leads past the farmhouse at Aberkin. The track emerges on the A497 Porthmadog to Pwllheli road. Cross at this point to take a path leading to Llanystumdwy, to emerge once again on the banks of the Afon Dwyfor at the centre of the village. Drop down for a spectacular view of the river as it flows under the bridge in the centre of the village. Llanystumdwy provides a choice of refreshment with a riverside café or the village inn close to the museum.

The modern day equivalent still serves the remote Lleyn Peninsula with daily services from Pwllheli to Machynlleth.

Opposite: BR Class Five 4-6-0 Black Five No 44871 seen here heading up *The Cambrian* from Machynlleth to Pwllheli. The locomotive designed by Sir William Stanier, the Chief Mechanical Engineer of the London, Midland and Scottish Railway, was built in 1945, eventually withdrawn from service after 23 years. 44871 secured its place in history taking part in the famous Fifteen Guinea Special, the last steam hauled mainline passenger train to run on British Rail on 11 August 1968.

Much time can be spent in the village, the former home to the first Welsh Prime Minister.

David Lloyd George would be remembered as a Welshman, but he was born in Manchester in the winter of 1863. His father became a farmer in Pembrokeshire but was to die when David was only seven months old. The family came to stay with his uncle here in the village of Llanystumdwy where they were to make their home. David qualified as a solicitor but always had desires in another field. Following a trip to London and The House of Commons David wrote, 'My supreme idea is to get on. To this idea I shall sacrifice everything – except I trust honesty. I am prepared to thrust even love itself under the wheels of my juggernaut if it obstructs the way'. He was elected to parliament in 1890. He rose to become Chancellor of the Exchequer in 1908, eight years later during World War One he became Prime Minister of the then coalition government. His achievements included the introduction of the old age pension and votes for women. Lloyd George was Prime Minister until 1922 and remained a member of parliament until his death in 1945. Winston Churchill spoke in 1945 describing him as 'a man of action, resource and creative energy'. He concluded: 'The greater part of our fortunes in war and peace were shaped by this one man'. The museum and Highgate Cottage where he spent his boyhood is dedicated to the life and times of David Lloyd George.

The memorial in the village dedicated to David Lloyd George.

Opposite: The Afon Dwyfor flows through the centre of the delightful historic village of LLanystumdwy creating a most enchanting aspect.

Highgate Cottage where David Lloyd George spent his boyhood, is dedicated to his life and times.

Spend some time to explore and appreciate the delightful village.

At the bridge follow the lane directly ahead past some cottages to locate a footpath into the wooded river bank to Lloyd George's last resting place and a memorial designed by Clough Ellis Williams, who as we discovered earlier designed and built Portmeirion.

Returning to the bridge take the road now on your left leading up towards the main Porthmadog road where you will find the museum.

After spending a while in Llanystumdwy the return journey begins by heading left from the museum to reach the A497. Turn left for a short distance then cross the road taking the track on your right that re-crosses the railway line by way of a bridge, then follows an enclosed stony track heading back to the coast.

At a fork in the track you can continue right to re-emerge on the banks of the Afon Dwyfor or turn left, passing the farm before the shoreline comes into view, a slightly shorter route. Whichever track you choose, you now retrace your outward steps back to Criccieth with fine views afforded of the castle and a magnificent backdrop of Snowdonia and Tremadog Bay.

The route back to Criccieth takes you past the museum.

The new marina is now said to be one of the best in Wales with berths available for over 400 boats and moorings available for overnight visitors.

PWLLHELI

Pwllheli, pronounced 'Per-thelly' is known as the unofficial capital of Llŷn with the large majority of the population speaking fluent Welsh. Pwllheli is a busy market town, in complete contrast to the many fishing villages and small inland settlements that have developed throughout the peninsula. The market, held every Wednesday in Y Maes, is said to be one of the busiest in Wales. The town, as would be expected, has a variety of retail shops, restaurants, a theatre and cinema.

Present day Pwllheli is popular with visitors for traditional beach holidays but also caters for walkers and cyclists, with the area around the town – as is the majority of the peninsula, designated as an Area of Outstanding Natural Beauty (AONB). Golfers are also well catered for, as are the sailing fraternity.

The new marina is now said to be one of the best in Wales, with berths for over 400 boats and moorings available for overnight visitors. The marina is owned by Gwynedd Council and the only sheltered harbour in the northern part of Cardigan Bay. The marina has hosted several major sailing events including the World Sailing Championships and local regattas.

The two beaches that span the town are the shingle sands of the South Beach that stretch out for over three miles toward Llanbedrog and Glan-y-mor a sandy beach that extends for a similar distance in the direction of Criccieth culminating at the small headland of Pen-y-chain.

An event in the 1940s was to have a significant impact on the town putting Pwllheli on the tourist map, having a far greater effect on tourism that the coming of the railways during the Victorian era.

The towns history can be traced back to 1355 when it received its charter as a borough, from Edward the Black Prince, with the market still held on the same day on Y Maes (the field). Shipbuilding and fishing, as you would expect, were to become the industrial backbone of the community. During the 1890s the town was developed by Solomon Andrews who oversaw the building of the promenade and began a period of house building at the towns west end. The Cambrian Coast Railway decided to build its northern terminus at Pwllheli, an act that was to open up the Llŷn to the early tourist industry. Having survived the Beeching axe in the 1960s and other attempts at closure, it is a delight to see the line still operating. The railway is a vital artery and a blessing for the tourists industry with daily services still running along the picturesque Cambrian Coast calling at Porthmadog, Harlech, Barmouth, Machynlleth and Shrewsbury.

A tramway ran, taking tourists further west to Llanbedrog, up until 1927 when a storm caused serious damage to a section of the track at Carreg y Defaid. The land was subsequently sold and the tramway tracks removed during the winter of 1928.

Pwllheli earned a place in Welsh history as the birthplace of Plaid Cymru, the Welsh Independence Party. Pwllheli has in the past hosted the National Eisteddfod, a competition celebrating Welsh music and art.

The war memorial that stands proudly in Ffordd Y Cob commemorates the residents of Pwllheli who were killed or missing during the two World Wars. Possibly the most poignant verse of a poem written by Laurence Binyon *For The Fallen* first published in 1914 is the following accolade;
'They shall grow not old, as we that are left grow old,
Age shall not weary them, nor the years condemn.
At the going down of the sun and in the morning
We will remember them'.

The event that put Pwllheli well and truly on the holiday map occurred a few miles to the east at Penychain, where Butlins were to establish a holiday camp. Billy Butlin opened his first holiday camp in 1936 in Skegness with a second soon following in Clacton. A third was under construction at Filey in 1939 but due to the outbreak of World War Two, the first two camps were given over to military use with Filey completed for the same purpose. An additional camp was built at Ayr. Billy was asked at the request of the government to construct a further camp in North Wales. An area of 150 acres of farmland was identified at Penychain less than four miles east of Pwllheli. The building of the camp began with a clause built in that Billy could buy the camp and the others back after the war. The site at Penychain was perfect for both military use and as a holiday resort as it borders the sea with the magnificent distant backdrop of Snowdonia. The site was relatively gentle sloping and had its own ready built railway halt at the heart of the complex.

Work began on what was to be known as HMS Glendower, a training base for the Admiralty and the Merchant Navy. Perhaps its most famous sailor to pass through was Philip Mountbatten now the Duke of Edinburgh, the Queen's husband. This was said to have led to a royal visit by HRH and the Queen to the camp in August 1963.

True to the clause at the end of hostilities, Billy Butlin bought the camps from the government with Filey opening in 1945 and both Skegness and Clacton following in 1946 and Ayr in 1947. Despite much opposition from local people and a public enquiry, the camp at Pwllheli also opened in 1947 with a capacity of 5,000, a figure that was to increase in its heyday to 8,000, the camp becoming a huge success. Post war all inclusive holidays were now available to the majority of families costing no more than the average weeks pay.

The site boasted its own miniature railway that transported guests from the camp to the coast – a distance of just under a mile. The railway began in 1953 and ran for 43 years closing in 1996, surviving ironically 30 years after the Beeching cuts. A chair lift began operating during the 1960s following the course of the railway providing a panoramic view for holiday makers. 1990 was to see the resort renamed Starcoast and is now known as Hafan y Mor, (Haven by the Sea) with most of the site redeveloped.

The lifeboat station at Pwllheli was established in 1891 with the building of a boathouse and a unique option of launching into the harbour or over the beach with the installation of doors at each end. 1930 was to witness the arrival of the stations first motor boat.

Opposite: Present day Pwllheli is popular with visitors for traditional beach holidays but also caters for the sailing fraternity.

LLANBEDROG

Llan takes it meaning from a settlement around a church and west of Pwllheli we arrive at the site of the church of St Pedrog, in the village of Llanbedrog. St Pedrog is believed to have originated from Cornwall and would almost certainly have built an early structure during the sixth century, perhaps on the site of the current church at the foot of Mynydd Tir-y-cwmwd or as it is also known, Llanbedrog Head. Legend has it that Pedrog was a prince who renounced his right to inherit his father's kingdom to become a monk on Bodmin. He left Cornwall travelling it is said by sea, the journey assumed from the presence of churches bearing his name in Pembrokeshire and Cardigan as well as here at Llanbedrog.

The current structure of St Pedrog dates from mediaeval times, with the present nave built during the 13th century. The chancel was added during the early 16th century, with restoration work carried out in the 19th century and again toward the latter part of the 20th century. It is believed that St Pedrog's once suffered damage at the hands of Cromwell's troops.

Llanbedrog is dominated by the bulk of Llanbedrog Head located to the west of the village, jutting out to sea, creating a clear division between Llanbedrog and its near neighbour Abersoch. The headland at Mynydd Tir-y-cwmwd covered in gorse and heather rises over 400ft above sea level. The summit plateau provides breathtaking views over Abersoch and eastward along the southern shore of Llŷn, taking in Pwllheli, Criccieth and the distant mountains of southern Snowdonia across Cardigan Bay.

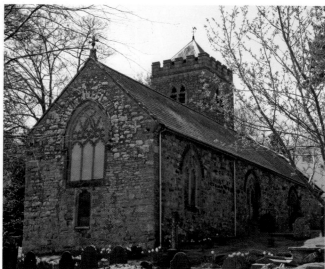

The current structure of the church of St Pedrog dates from mediaeval times.

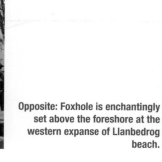

Opposite: Foxhole is enchantingly set above the foreshore at the western expanse of Llanbedrog beach.

Ordnance Survey data © Crown copyright and database right 2012

Llanbedrog Head is criss-crossed by many paths and at the foot of the cliffs are the remains of pre war granite quarries. From the beach at low tide the remains of a jetty can be seen, once used by ships to transport stone from the quarries. The sandy beach at Llanbedrog is delightful, nestled below the headland and backed by trees creating a perfect idyll. During the summer months a characteristic row of brightly painted wooden beach huts provide the finishing touches to the summer scene.

During the latter part of the 19th and into the early 20th century the horse drawn tramway operated between Pwllheli and Llanbedrog. The purpose was to cater for early tourists allowing them to travel further west than Pwllheli, a town that was experiencing the beginning of the tourist boom, a legacy of the Victorian era of railway building.

Llanbedrog is home to some early dwellings closely allied as being quintessentially Welsh cottages, low single story structures, at times with several cottages forming a terrace. Construction was usually by means of rubble stone, sometimes rendered with the eves at door height and would most likely have been thatched before slates became the order of the day.

LLANBEDROG HEAD (MYNYDD TIR-Y-CWMWD) WALK

Distance 3 miles, with an estimated time of 2–2.5 hours.

A walk to the summit plateau, where the breathtaking views are a generous reward for the modest climb. Situated at the north-east side of the headland is a statue *The Weary Traveller* known as the Iron Man. The present Iron Man replaced an earlier Tin Man, who in turn had replaced a wooden figure head, from a ship that had sunk in the bay.

The walk is perhaps best started from the National Trust car park in the village, where ample refreshment options will be available for your return. Park in the car park at grid reference 331 314 down the lane that leads to the sea (charges apply). The distance and time are approximate for this short walk, as you may want to explore the summit to a greater or lesser degree.

Opposite: The colourful row of beach huts adds to the quintessential charm of this delightful seaside village.

65

Leave the car park turning right heading upwards passing the church before bearing left onto a small lane, Craig y Llan. The initial part of the lane is very steep, but remembering this is part of the ascent of the 400ft high plateau, the lane walking makes for a relatively easy climb. The hedgerows are abundant with wild flowers echoing most of the peninsula's quiet country lanes. The lane is narrow but occasional traffic can take advantage of a few passing places, much akin to the Highlands and Islands of Scotland. Continue along the quiet lane, all the while increasing in height, for just under half a mile before bearing left following a lane ascending the hillside.

In a short distance at a T junction bear left past a cottage on the corner following a track past some more cottages before joining a footpath. The path initially descends for a short while before joining the main footpath from Llanbedrog which we now follow bearing right climbing through some trees. This is another relatively short, but

steep section, to reach the heather and gorse clad headland. Continue on where the path leads ahead to the triangulation pillar away to your right. The summit now boasts a 'toposcope' allowing easier identification of the distant mountains of Snowdonia and a couple of sturdy wooden seats for a well deserved rest.

The summit now boasts a 'toposcope' allowing easier identification of the distant mountains of Snowdonia.

The entire sweep of the southern coast of Llŷn is now set out before you. To the east, Moel-y-Gest rises high above Porthmadog and Criccieth Castle stands proud on its rocky promontory. The bustling town of Pwllheli seems within touching distance, with magnificent stretches of sand on its flanks shimmering in the summer sun as the azure sea laps at the gently shelving coast.

To the west the vast expanse of dune backed golden sands that front The Warren holiday park, eventually yield to the popular village of Abersoch. The western extreme of Porth Neigwl (Hell's Mouth) and inland to Mynytho and Windmill Hill, with the backdrop of Carn Fadryn, complete an awe inspiring scene from the summit of Mynydd Tir-y-cwmwd, a mere 420ft above sea level.

The summit of Mynydd Tir-y-cwmwd, a mere 420ft above sea level.

Opposite: Turn left at the cottage onto a track leading toward the heather-clad headland. The lane is narrow but occasional traffic can take advantage of a few passing places, In spring the hedgerows become abundant with wild flowers. Wild Garlic produces leafless flower stems during spring, smelling strongly of garlic when crushed.

The present iron man is hollow unlike his predecessor the Tin Man and 'sings' when the wind blows.

The magnificent panorama encompasses Cardigan Bay and the mountainous West coast of Wales.

Bright yellow gorse transforms the headland during spring and will occasionally come into flower during a mild winter.

The magnificent panorama will lure you to stay a while, nevertheless when ready to move on, take the path heading north east from the triangulation pillar in the direction of the wide sweep of Llanbedrog beach.

Descending the heather clad slopes you will eventually reach the Iron Man on a rocky promontory at grid reference 333 311.

From here an alternative short cut back to the car park can be taken by descending the very steep steps a little to the north-west of the statue that emerge onto the beach at Llanbedrog, before following the road Lon Nant-Lago back up towards the car park.

The present statue was winched into position by helicopter in 2002 and was crafted by local blacksmiths David and Hugh Jones. The present Iron Man is hollow unlike his predecessor the Tin Man, and is said to sing when the wind blows. The original wooden figure head was erected in 1919 and stood on the site for almost 60 years.

This collection of coins can be seen if you take the short descent from the summit.

Looking east to Pwllheli.

The main walk now continues following the path around the headland above the disused quarries. The cliffs are extremely dangerous at this point and extreme care is needed. Continue around the headland with views opening up west along the glorious stretch of sand that fronts The Warren, to the village of Abersoch some 2 miles distant.

Head all the while inland following a distinctive path that becomes a track. Continue on the track passing some cottages on the left to rejoin the quiet lane that brought you from Llanbedrog. At the end of the lane turn right passing the church now on your right, all the while heading towards the sea to find the car park.

The sandy beach below the head is punctuated by rocks revealing a myriad of seaweed at low tide.

'Foxhole' is located in an idyllic setting.

At low tide the rocky coastline is exposed, the view enhanced by the distant Cadair Idris range.

The time and distance covered on this walk will have been down to how much of the headland you want to visit and how much time is spent soaking up the wonderful views. The village does provide several options for refreshment with both The Ship Inn and Glyn-y-Weddw Arms, and a selection of tea rooms and restaurants, to help refresh you after a most exhilarating short walk.

Delightful cottages line the roadside as our journey continues westward from Llanbedrog to our next destination close to the village of Mynytho.

Quintessentially Welsh cottages are low single-storey structures, at times with several cottages forming a terrace.

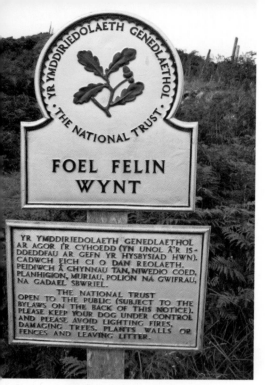

FOEL FAWR

Foel Felin (Windmill Hill)

Sitting above the village of Mynytho and overlooking Llanbedrog Head is a circular tower, the remains of an old windmill on Foel Fawr known locally as the 'Jam Pot'. The National Trust sign points the way at grid reference 306 319 where there is a small parking area at the side of the narrow lane. The sign reads Foel Felin Wynt, Felin Wynt, translated means Windmill Hill. Foel is a name describing a bare summit.

There is some debate to the towers history, one theory suggesting that it was struck several times by lightning, while others suggest it was never a productive site due to wind shear, caused by sudden changes in the direction and speed of the prevailing wind. It is estimated that over 10,000 windmills were in operation throughout Britain during the 19th century but the birth of the industrial revolution rendered many surplus to requirements, their power replaced by steam. It is perhaps ironic that 200 years later, we are now seeing a rise in the development of wind power with offshore wind farms along the North Wales coast.

To reach the tower requires a fairly steep, but short ascent from the National Trust sign, but the views afforded from the bare summit are well worth the effort. To the east are the distinct peaks of Yr Eifl and beyond, the mountains of the Snowdonia National Park.

South provides a panorama along the coast of Llŷn taking in the headland of Abersoch and St Tudwal's islands, Llanbedrog Head, and further east, Pwllheli with the magnificent views continuing across Cardigan Bay to the Cadair Idris range in Mid Wales. If the weather conditions are clear, the mountains of Ireland can be seen in the far west.

Opposite:
The National Trust sign confirms that you are close to the summit of Foel Fawr.

The hedgerows and stone walls are a haven for wild flowers during the summer months.

Looking east encompasses the distant peaks of Yr Eifl, and the western fringes of the Snowdonia National Park from the elevated summit of Foel Fawr, 60ft above sea level.

The entrance to the old mill reveals very little evidence of past activity, but the tower is to be found in a good state of repair.

ABERSOCH

Nautical Lady **waiting for the tide to turn, safe at anchor within the harbour walls at Abersoch.**

Leaving Llanbedrog we edge closer to the lands end of Wales. The main road, the A499 from Pwllheli, terminates at Abersoch, the remainder of the journey on unclassified and B roads helping to maintain the remote feel to this area of Llŷn. In the late 1700s just a handful of buildings and a mill were clustered around the estuary making up the small village. Abersoch grew with the arrival of miners during the late 19th century. Lead was mined at Llanengan with many Cornish miners arriving in the area, several staying after the mining ceased to make Llŷn their home. Some of the original mine buildings still remain as evidence of the lead workings.

The early 20th century saw tourists begin to arrive but on a small scale, not until the latter part of the century did the excellent beaches and good sailing boost its popularity. Now a major tourist attraction, the once thriving fishing village of Abersoch is aided by its excellent location, being sheltered from the prevailing winds.

With its golden sands and shallow shelving waters Abersoch is popular with both families and the sailing fraternity, and is now one of Britain's most important sailing centres. As with any coastal areas, property prices are significantly higher than the regional average.

This salubrious assembly of beach huts bordering the sand dunes form a colourful backdrop to the south beach at Abersoch.

The value of property was perhaps highlighted more so when a beach hut was sold for a staggering £85,000 in 2008, one of 200 on the main beach at Abersoch, although it did come with its own patch of sand dune! A mobile home was reported for sale in 2007 for £500,000 at the nearby Warren holiday park.

The village takes its name from the Afon Soch an extraordinary river with regard of its journey to the sea. The source of the Afon Soch is close to the prehistoric burial site of Mynydd Cefnamwlch some 6 miles north west, close to the northern coast of Llŷn. The river meanders south on its journey to the sea close to Hell's Mouth but takes an almost right angled turn north east to follow a glacial gorge to reach the sea at Abersoch.

Located south of Abersoch are the two small islands of St Tudwal's. The largest, St Tudwal's East, is home to the remains of a Priory. Tradition has it that St Tudwal lived on the island during the sixth century: no doubt helped by a natural spring that exists to provide fresh water.

Trinity House erected a lighthouse on St Tudwal's West in 1877. The lighthouse is 36ft high with its light set some 150ft above the sea with a range of 14 nautical miles. The light was automated in 1922 and updated in 1995 to make use of solar power. What is the disparity between a nautical and a statute land mile is often the question asked. A mile on land is 1,760 yards whereas a nautical mile used for all air and sea travel is 2,026 yards, the calculation taking account of the curvature of the earth.

Abersoch retains its tradition as an important fishing village.

Opposite: The harbour at Abersoch provides a safe haven for a diversity of boats.

The church dedicated to St Tegonwy is an unusual design as the base of the tower is octagonal with the upper portion cylindrical.

LLANDEGWNING

Restoration work on the church was carried out in the early 19th century. *The Imperial Gazetteer of England and Wales 1872*, however, described the church at Llandegwning as such, 'Dedicated to St Tegonwy and was in a state of disrepair'. An unusual design as the base of the tower is octagonal with the upper portion cylindrical. Llandegwning can be found some 3 miles north west of Abersoch just over a mile from the coast of Hell's Mouth. Worth a visit, found within a splendid rural setting bordering a quiet country lane.

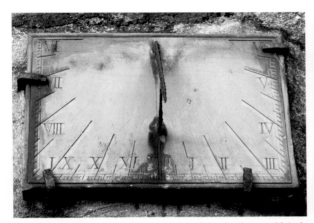

The origin of the sundial almost certainly dates back to prehistoric times when stone rows or circles were used as astrological calendars.

Over many centuries the sundial was used to tell the time becoming a prominent architectural feature on many churches and one can still be seen today on the church at Llandegwning. The origin of the sundial almost certainly dates back to prehistoric times when stone rows or circles were used as astrological calendars. The sundial operates on the basis that the shadow of the gnomon or pointer moves from one side to the other as the sun moves across the sky during the day. The earliest mechanical clocks required sundials alongside to adjust their rather inaccurate time keeping. As late as the 1800s the sundial was gradually being replaced as the recognised timepiece with the advent of the mechanical clock becoming more accurate and readily available.

Late winter sun serves to highlight the octagonal tower.

81

LLANGIAN

The pretty village of Llangian stands at a confluence of quiet country roads leading to Mynytho, Llanengan, Botwnnog and Rhiw, and has remained largely untouched by tourism, the village being a notable winner of the award for the tidiest village in Wales. The village still retains a post office and shop. The church at Llangian stands in a hollow nestled beside a tributary of the Afon Soch some two miles north-west from Abersoch.

The entrance to the beautifully located church is through a traditional lychgate. The word lych evolves from Saxon times, meaning corpse: as the lychgate was the traditional place where a corpse would be laid out. In the Middle Ages most people would be buried in unadorned shrouds and the priest would conduct the first part of the burial service under the shelter of the lychgate.

The earliest records date the church from the 13th century but it is believed a church may have stood on this site even earlier. The west end of the church dates from this time, the original doorways now blocked. Further building work took place during the 15th century with the present structure being completed after repairs carried out in the 19th century with the inclusion of the west door and the impressive porch.

The church is dedicated to Cian who was said to have been a servant of St Peris the founder of Llanberis. In the church yard, on the south side close to the sundial, is a small erect pillar known as a funery monument of the fifth or sixth century. A Latin inscription on the stone commemorates Melus the doctor. The inscription is in three vertical lines reading 'MELI MEDICI /FILI MARTINI/I (a) CIT'; 'THE STONE OF MELUS THE DOCTOR SON OF MARTINUS HE LIES HERE'. The stone is believed to be unique in Britain being the only record of a medicus on an early Christian epitaph as the profession of the deceased would not normally be mentioned, although such practise was common place on pagan Roman epitaphs. The stone is said to confirm evidence of contact during the early mediaeval period with influences from other coastal areas around the Irish Sea where reference may have been made to a priest on epitaphs but not a reference to a doctor. It is unclear if the stone is standing at its original site.

Dating from the fifth or sixth century the stone is believed to be unique in Britain being the only record of a medicus on an early Christian epitaph.

Opposite: The origin of the lychgate dates from Saxon times and would almost certainly have been used by the priest to conduct the first part of a funeral service, the roof providing shelter.

The church at Llanengan lies less than a mile inland from Porth Neigwl and is unique as it is the only church on Llŷn with a complete view of Bardsey Island.

LLANENGAN CHURCH

The church at Llanengan lies less than a mile in land from Porth Neigwl and one and a half miles south-west from Abersoch. Llanengan Church has a notable connection with the Abbey of St Mary on Ynys Enlli (Bardsey) and is unique – being the only church on Llŷn that has a complete view of Bardsey Island. The structure dates from the late 15th to the early 16th century, with the present tower being added during the latter period.

St Engan's or St Einion was restored during the mid 19th century with additional repairs carried out in the 1930s and more recently during the late 20th century. St Einion is reputed to be one of the oldest and prettiest churches on the peninsula.

Above the west doorway is an inscription in raised letters, 'This belfry was built in honour of St Einion, King of Wales, Apostle of the Scots AD 1534' recording the building of the tower in 1534.

Inside the church there is an ancient chest known as 'Cyff Engan' hewed from a solitary block of timber and is bound. The lid contains a large slot for coins and is believed to date from mediaeval times.

Tradition has it that the tower's three bells were brought over to the mainland from the Abbey of St Mair on Bardsey, with the inscriptions dated 1624 and two inscribed with the words 'St. Einion Rex Wallia et Actus Scotorum'. There is a holy well, Ffynnon Einion Sant, nearby.

The Yew is a feature of Churchyards throughout Wales. The Yew tree has always been held sacred and linked with death and rebirth. In ancient times its heart wood was used for making the Welsh longbow. The flat, dark green leaves are poisonous, as are most parts of the tree, including the seeds but, surprisingly, the bright red fruits surrounding the seeds are not and have been used as laxatives.

Legend has it that several Celtic leaders would have used Yew to poison themselves rather than surrender to the Romans. Yews are traditionally found in churchyards partly because of their life span, with many predating the churchyards they now stand in. The oldest recorded in Europe is in Fortingall Churchyard, Loch Tay, Scotland, reputed to be over 3,000 years old with a circumference of 56ft.

Tradition has it that they would have been used as Pagan burial sites, perhaps one reason being, that cattle would have been discouraged from grazing around the area. The ancient theory of rebirth continues as medicinally a chemotherapy drug Pacilitaxel can be extracted from the common Yew.

During late winter through to early spring, the male tree produces small catkins with the pollen distributed on the wind. The female tree will begin to fruit during summer with the bright red berries in full bloom by mid September.

The Yew is a feature of churchyards throughout Wales having always been held sacred and linked with death and rebirth.

85

The wide open expanse of Porth Neigwl lays directly in the path of storm force south-westerly winds, not only does it provide a paradise for surfers, but a delightful feeling of a wild remote place for the photographer on stormy days.

Llanengan began to develop from a small fishing village in the early 1800s and by 1860 the population had increased due to the influx of workers and their families at the nearby lead mines. The Tanrallt lead mines were productive until the end of the century. With very little industrial activity since then it has allowed the area to retain its quintessential remote 'Llŷn' character. The lead was mined outside of the village where a chimney can still be seen today from the road to Porth Neigwl (Hell's Mouth) marking the entrance to the former mine and was used as a ventilation shaft.

PORTH NEIGWL

Porth Neigwl witnessed over 20 shipwrecks between 1820 and 1920, not surprisingly, being open to south-westerly gales. An area dreaded by ancient mariners returning home. Today Porth Neigwl is popular with surfers due to its very large waves and gently shelving beach boosted at times by very strong south-westerly winds. The beach is made up of mostly medium sized pebbles but at low tide a large expanse of sand is revealed. The currents, however, need to be respected as the undertow can be significant during rough weather.

The expanse of the beach begins a short distance east of Rhiw where magnificent views are obtained from the elevated ground encompassing the entire panorama of the beach running as it does almost four miles to its southern extent, a mile south from Llanengan. The Llŷn coastal path follows above the beach on the cliffs. The beach falls within an Area of Outstanding Natural Beauty (AONB), has been designated Heritage Coast and forms part of a Site of Special Scientific Interest (SSSI).

From a solely picturesque perspective I would say that the best views are found looking out to sea on perhaps wild stormy days when the sea is in its most turbulent state.

The narrow lanes of Llŷn are a delight to walk or cycle, but are not suitable for all traffic as this unusual warning sign shows, confirming that perhaps map reading should still be seen as an essential skill in the countryside.

The sign confirms you are at Porth Neigwl (Hell's Mouth).

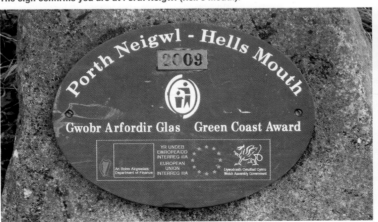

An awe inspiring sunrise looking south-east across Aberdaron Bay to the headland of Trwyn y Penrhyn, the islands of Ynys Gwylan-fawr and Ynys Gwylan-bach shrouded in storm clouds.

ABERDARON

Aberdaron stands on the shore in a small valley at the confluence of the Afon Daron and Afon Cyll-y-felin, taking its name from the Afon Daron. Aberdaron was the last resting stop for pilgrims on route to Bardsey Island (Ynys Enlli), the island of 20,000 saints. The 14th-century Y Gegin Fawr (the old kitchen) provided food and water before the last 2 miles of their journey by boat to the island. Y Gegin Fawr still continues its tradition, as today it serves as a tea room for 21st-century travellers.

One site dominates the village standing above the shore on the pilgrims route to Bardsey. St Hywyn's Church was built in the 12th century although it is believed a building has stood on this site since the sixth century.

St Hywyn's Church dominates the village standing above the shore on the pilgrim's route to Bardsey. The church is jointly dedicated to St Lleuddad and St Hywyn who arrived on Bardsey in the sixth century. St Hywyn's is also home to the Anelog Stones, a pair of sixth-century grave stones. The two stones were found at Capel Anelog on the eastern slope of Mynydd Anelog.

The church has a Norman door and north nave from the same period, with a square bell tower. The south nave was added during the prosperous 15th century. In 1841 the church was abandoned when a new church was built in the village, a move that was to prove unpopular with the congregation, who returned to 'the cathedral of Llŷn' as it is known, in 1906.

Aberdaron is the quintessential Welsh seaside village, a beautiful place with a delightful collection of cottages clustered on the hillside above a long golden beach. Originally a fishing village and remaining much as it would have it retains its Celtic language as part of everyday life. A delightful 17th-century stone bridge crosses the Afon Daron in the centre of the village. The arrival of the railways in the 19th century opened up the Llŷn but never reached Aberdaron helping to retain its remote feel at the lands end of Wales.

These delightful corrugated iron-clad buildings create a sense of timelessness.

Opposite: The remains of the old pier at Porth Simdde. The Afon Saint flows into the sea from its source on the slopes of Mynydd Anelog. During the late 19th century a jetty was built to service the nearby mineral works at Gwaith Pompren although it is said the jetty was never used for its intended purpose.

The 14th-century Y Gegin Fawr (the old kitchen) provided food and water for the pilgrims before the last leg of their journey across the treacherous waters of Bardsey Sound.

A shaft of sunlight creates an impression of a silver sea with Ynys Gwylan-fawr silhouetted against the stormy skies.

Thomas Pennant, the traveller and writer, visited in the 18th century telling of it as 'a poor village' but by the early 1900s travel guides were telling of 'the remotest and quaintest village on Lleyn' and of 'the salubrious sea and mountain breezes'. The village had two hotels with local farmhouses providing additional accommodation to supplement their incomes. Tourism had begun.

During the late 1700s as with several coastal locations on Llŷn, Aberdaron was to witness shipbuilding on the beach. The last ship to have been built at Aberdaron was the sloop *Victory* in 1792. Smuggling, as one would expect, has played a large part in the area's history, being located on such a remote stretch of coast, tales of wrecking have also been told. It is said that a French ship unloaded illicit brandy at Aberdaron in the late 1700s attempting to sell its cargo to the locals. A schooner on route to Scotland was said to have offloaded tea, brandy and gin nearby in 1824.

With such strong traditions as a fishing village it is no surprise that many still earn their living from the sea, some running pleasure trips around the beautiful Llŷn coast, while fishing still continues from the cove at Porth Meudwy.

The landscape of Llŷn with its patchwork of fields and quiet country lanes is perhaps more evident here than anywhere else on the peninsula. The fields are enclosed by banks of earth and stone topped by gorse and bracken.

Y Gegin Fawr still continues its tradition.

Y Gegin Fawr
The Big Kitchen
BUILT 1300 A.D. WHERE THE SAINTS COULD CLAIM A MEAL BEFORE CROSSING THE SOUND TO BARDSEY ISLAND.

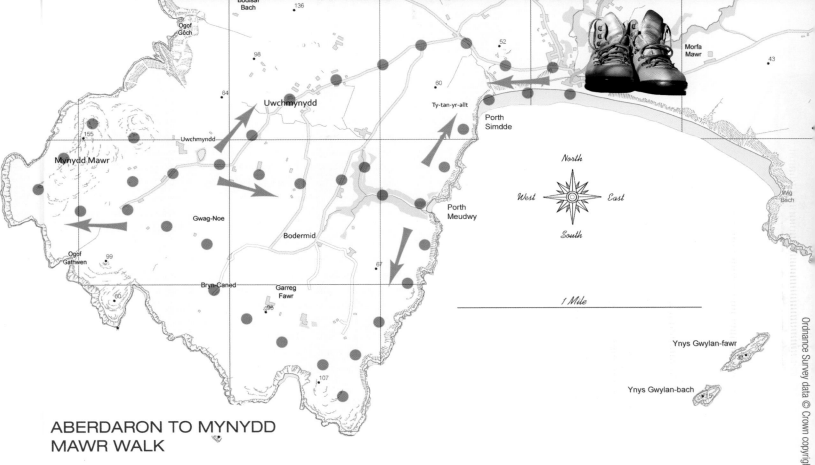

North

West   East

South

1 Mile

ABERDARON TO MYNYDD MAWR WALK

Distance 8 miles, with an estimated time of 5 hours.

A rewarding coastal walk can be taken from Aberdaron to Mynydd Mawr, the lands end of Llŷn. The views on route are superb taking in both the north and south coasts and across to Bardsey Island. Inland the views are no less impressive as the patchwork of vivid green fields and isolated farms unfold to reveal the classic Llŷn landscape The walk can be completed in 5 hours although taking in the views could add some considerable time.

From the beach in front of Gwesty Ty Newydd turn right to walk to Porth Simdde where the remains of the old pier can still be seen at low tide. The pier was built during the early 20th century. Steps lead up the cliff at Porth Simdde where you bear left to follow the coastal path sign posted to Porth Meudwy.

Once atop the cliffs continue on the coastal path that wends its way over the gorse covered cliffs and provides spectacular views east to Aberdaron and the islands of Ynys Gwylan-fawr and Ynys Gwylan-bach. The island closest to the coast is Ynys Gwylan-fawr, 'fawr' meaning big and 'bach' meaning small. The islands are home to a thriving colony of puffins during the breeding season, somewhat helped by their isolation from the mainland. Pass through a metal gate to drop down into Porth Meudwy.

The tiny inlet was used in the middle ages by pilgrims embarking on the last leg of their journey across the hazardous Bardsey Sound to Ynys Enlli. Today the cove is a busy lobster port used by the local fisherman and is the nearest safe departure point for Bardsey Island.

This delightful walk continues by climbing the steps on the westward cliffs to once again reach the cliff top. The walking is now straightforward but care is needed as this section of the path is deteriorating in places as you negotiate your way above steep cliff edges of the numerous coves. Once past the last cove of Hen Borth, at the fork take the right hand path keeping a wall on your left. Head across open grassland to reach the rocky headland of Pen y Cil to be rewarded with outstanding views to Bardsey Island across the treacherous waters of Bardsey Sound, care is again needed as there is a sheer drop to the water below. These treacherous waters have been responsible for countless shipwrecks. In 1914 a schooner hit a rock and sank, the cargo of china clay from Cornwall was lost, but every single one of the crew survived.

On reaching the cairn on Pen y Cil a path now leads you northwards crossing a ladder stile before taking a clearly sign posted path on the left, guiding you in the direction of the distant Mynydd Mawr. You are now on National Trust land at Mynydd Bychestyn. The route continues keeping the wall on your right along a grassy path passing through a metal gate before taking a right turn along a well defined enclosed track. Continue taking another left turn through a metal gate and crossing another ladder stile. Follow the track to the top of the field through an additional gate then keep a bank on your left following another track, in due course emerging onto a lane.

Porth Meudwy is a busy lobster port used by local fisherman, and a safe departure point for Bardsey Island.

The coastal waters around Mynydd Mawr.

Outstanding views to Bardsey Island (Ynys Enlli), the island of 20,000 saints across the treacherous waters of Bardsey Sound are afforded from the slopes of Mynydd Mawr.

Once on the lane, turn left crossing a cattle grid to follow the path to the headland of Braich y Pwll, and the remains of St Mary's Chapel. You are now at the true lands end of North Wales. Once again superb views of Bardsey Island can be taken in from this point. The important site of the chapel of St Mary's is close by, having been one of the last ports of call where prayers were offered for the safe passage of pilgrims on the last leg of their journey to Ynys Enlli. Further down the cliffs St Mary's Well can be found, reputed to have been blessed by the Virgin Mary. The well is a cleft in the rocks below the high tide level. A visit to the well should only be attempted at low tide and requires a degree of agility to negotiate the perilous cliffs. Legend has it that the well has the ability to purify itself, even after the salt waters of the highest of tides and storm tossed seas have become immersed with the pure waters of the well.

Continue in a north westerly direction climbing steps toward the summit of Mynydd Mawr just above the site of the World War Two radar station. This was an important strategic point and was home to many military personnel during the war. The positioning of the radar station was to counter the fear that the coast of Ireland could be used to guide enemy ships and aircraft, should they launch a night time attack on the Welsh coast. As a neutral country Ireland did not have a blackout imposed.

The patchwork of fields and farmsteads of Llŷn are no more apparent than here on the summit of Mynydd Mawr.

The heather clad slopes of Mynydd Mawr provide a contrasting foreground as the view continues eastward encompassing Carn Fadryn and Yr Eifl.

From the summit you are rewarded with outstanding views eastward along the entire Lleyn Peninsula encompassing the distant mountains of Snowdonia. The view continues north to Caernarfon Bay and south to Cardigan Bay. In addition, given the right weather conditions, you are rewarded with views west to the distant Wicklow Mountains of Ireland.

The summit is home to the old Coastguard Station with commanding views over Bardsey Sound. For over 80 years the building was the lookout for the Coastguard but, with the increasing advance of satellite technology in the early 1990s, the building was rendered redundant. The National Trust look after this distinctive part of Llŷn conserving the important heath-land habitat as well as maintaining the traditional Llŷn earth banks between the patchwork of fields to help preserve and encourage wildlife. As in other upland areas of Britain, ponies have been introduced to control the vegetation. From the summit a concrete road begins the descent, first heading north east before a series of twists and turns, winding its way down crossing the cattle grid to emerge on the lane where you first began the path to St Mary's Chapel and Braich y Pwll.

You now have two options, one is a delightful easy going stroll along pleasant country lanes walking a distance of some 2 miles back to Aberdaron. The second option is to continue on the lane for half a mile where the road bears sharp left, take the track straight ahead past farm buildings to continue across a field. Continue across another field to climb a ladder stile heading for a metal gate. Continue down some steps to follow a track that emerges onto a lane. Once on the lane turn right for a very short distance before steps ascend to a path that runs along the top of a typical Llŷn earth bank. Follow atop the earth bank dividing the patchwork of fields to emerge onto another lane. Turn left to follow the lane and in a short while you will reach a track on your right at Cwrt that descends to the cove of Porth Meudwy. From here you then retrace your outward steps taking the cliff path now on your left to return to Aberdaron.

If you have decided to continue on the easier route back to Aberdaron you are rewarded with easy walking on quiet country lanes. Bordered for the most part with the archetypal Llŷn stone and earth bank topped with gorse and bracken, the banks display an infinite variety of wild flowers through the different seasons. Excellent views of the Llŷn are afforded and the destination of Aberdaron unfolds as you begin to descend to the tiny village clinging to the hillside above the golden sands of Aberdaron Bay.

The lane back to Aberdaron takes you past these delightful whitewashed cottages.

The coastal path is well signposted and provides an 84 mile route from Caernarfon to Porthmadog.

The lanes of Llŷn are awash with wild flowers, during late summer the hedgerows are dotted with the nodding heads of the Harebell.

The stile leads the way back to Porth Meudwy if taking the longer route back to Aderdaron.

Late evening light allows Carn Fadryn, dominating the scene at the centre of Llŷn and the distant peak of Yr Eifl to stand proud.

The words to describe a view can occasionally be overstated but that would not be the case here as you look north-east from the slopes of Mynydd Anelog to the bulk of Carn Fadryn, set almost at the heart of Llŷn. Carn Fadryn dominates the village of Garnfadryn and has witnessed at least three periods of ancient hill fort building, while beyond lies the summit of the Lleyn Peninsula, Yr Eifl. Anglicised by English visitors as The Rivals, the striking mountain mass dominates the north coast, giving views from the summit as far south as St David's Head in Pembrokeshire. There are three peaks, the highest standing 1,849ft above sea level.

The Llŷn is dotted with tiny hamlets and villages, all connecting a patchwork of farms and fields that, until the coming of new technologies, were in the main isolated from the outside world. The postal service was at times the only contact beyond the shores of Llŷn. The first mail coach service was introduced in 1785 operating between Manchester, Liverpool, Portsmouth, Birmingham, Holyhead and Hereford to London. The mail coach also carried passengers but it was designed for speed and not comfort, with four seated inside and a further two carried on the roof. The first post boxes were introduced in Britain from 1853, some 13 years after the introduction of the first postage stamp, the 'Penny Black'. Prior to the introduction of postage stamps all mail had to be taken to the post office and the appropriate fee paid. The cipher on a post box identifies the period of installation. The post box that serves the area close to Rhoshirwaun bears the cipher GR and dates installation between 1910–36 during the reign of King George V.

The cipher GR dates installation during the reign of King George V.

PORTH OER (WHISTLING SANDS)

Porth Oer is to be found by turning left off the minor road just over 2 miles north of Aberdaron. The north western shores of Llŷn offers a far more rugged coastal landscape in contrast to the south, with numerous, undisturbed tiny coves, several only accessible on foot. The rocky cliffs drop down to the shore and are transformed with a carpet of thrift during early summer. The first sandy beach we encounter on the north western coast is Porth Oer, a splendid sheltered bay, also known as whistling sands. The name derives from the sound the dry sand creates when walked upon. Scientific tests have shown that the sand particles are rounded furthest from the sea, unlike a conventional sandy beach where the particles are random shapes. The regularity of the dry sand particles allow movement over each other in a uniform way thus creating the unique squeak or whistling sound.

PORTH OER TO MYNYDD ANELOG WALK

Distance 5 miles, with an estimated time of 3.5 hours.

A satisfying walk begins at Port Oer, with spectacular coastal scenery your constant companion for most of the journey. The first part of the walk follows the headlands to the west of Porth Oer where delightful coves await; some pleasurable lane walking then transports you to the foot of Mynydd Anelog.

Your reward, for the modest ascent of Mynydd Anelog, are the breathtaking views south to the lands end of Wales, and eastward along the entire peninsula to Yr Eifl. The return to Porth Oer retraces your steps back to Bryn Du farm then continues along the quiet country lane back to the car park. An alternative, if time permits, would be to head back to the cliff path taking the track on your left at the farm to follow the headland back to Porth Oer.

Opposite: Porth Oer is a splendid sheltered bay also known as 'whistling sands'. The name derives from the sound the dry sand creates when walked upon.

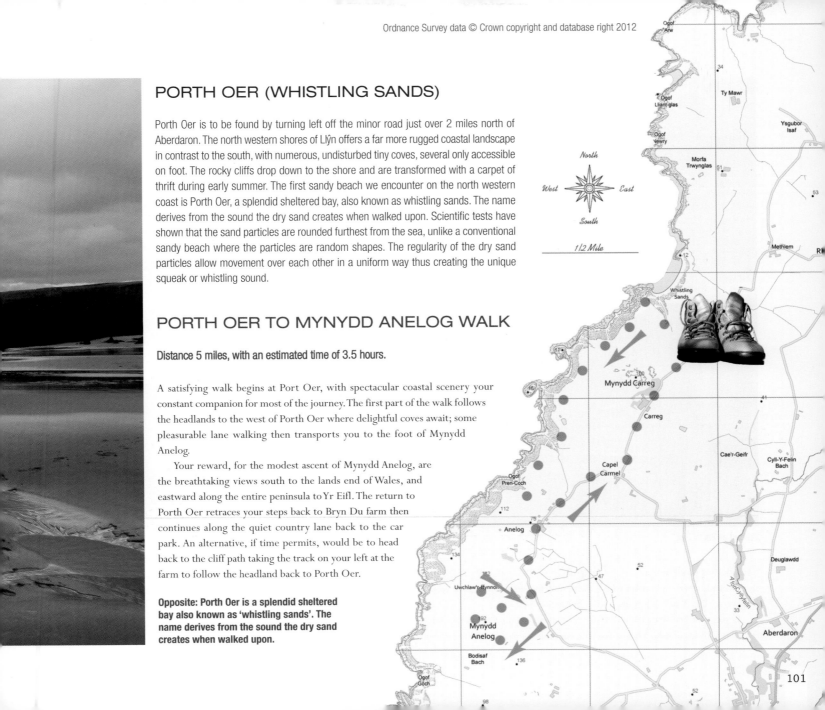

101

Sunset at Porth Oer.

From the National Trust car park grid reference 166 295, follow the lane down to the beach where a path on your left will lead you to the cliffs. Continue following the cliff path where, in a short while, the first of the small coves come into view, Dinas Bach. Evidence suggests that the headlands of Dinas Bach (small) and its neighbour Dinas Fawr (big) were once Iron Age fortified sites.

As you continue along the cliff top, the headland of Dias Fawr comes into view where a winch on the headland reveals that the small cove below is sometimes frequented by small fishing boats. The path continues descending to the tranquil cove of Porthorion.

Dramatic seascapes occur along the north coast.

In 1880 things were not as peaceful off the coat of Porthorion when 25 people lost their lives one terrible night. The 500 tonne sailing ship *Newry* had set sail from Warren Point, Ireland with almost four hundred emigrants bound for Quebec, Canada. The captain had elected to go south due to prevailing winds. The winds strengthened, forcing the ship towards Llŷn where she struck the rocks off Porthorion. Captain Crosby's orders were to abandon ship using the main mast as a bridge to safety. The crew had deserted the passengers, leaving them to the mercy of the captain, the ships mate and a sailor. It is said that it took over 10 hours to evacuate the ship. The Captain, his mate and the sailor bravely assisted by three local men, saved the lives of 375 men, women and children.

The path ahead of Porthorion gains height with the destination of Mynydd Anelog coming into view as the path heads inland through a small valley, crossing a stile to follow a clear track. Continue crossing another stile at Bryn Du farm where the track will bring you to the lane. Turn right onto the winding lane negotiating a sharp left hand bend before reaching a track that rises away to your right, the start of the ascent of Mynydd Anelog.

Pass the cottage and farm buildings going through the gate taking the track rising upward on your right at the fork. Follow the sheep track to the corner of the field taking a sharp right at the first cottage heading up past the second. Take a while to admire the weathervane atop the second cottage. The final ascent is somewhat steep, but relatively easy going, to reach the summit cairn, 628ft above sea level.

On the slopes of Mynydd Anelog experimental plots have been created to discover how best to conserve the heather habitat for the future. However, it is the past history that has a story to tell. Gors Anelog on the eastern slopes was the site of Capel Anelog, a long lost Celtic Monastery, perhaps the dawn of Christianity on Llŷn. No remains of the site are to be found, however, during the 18th century two gravestones dating from the sixth century were discovered. The slabs are inscribed in Latin with the translation revealing 'Veracius the priest lies here' and 'Senacus the priest lies here with the multitude of brethren priests'. The stones are now on display, housed in the church at Aberdaron.

The view from the summit is awesome, taking in Mynydd Mawr and across Bardsey Sound to Ynys Enlli (Bardsey Island). Ireland can be seen to the west given the right weather conditions while both the north and south coasts of Llŷn are set out before you. You may be compelled to rest here a while watching the waves crash into the rugged coast of Porth Llanllawen.

The cairn atop Mynydd Anelog at grid reference 151 272.

The path passes Craft Cottage beneath the summit of Mynydd Anelog; from this point the fascinating weathervane confirms you are looking south to Bardsey Island.

The descent can be taken by first heading north west to pick up a path, subsequently doubling back until the last cottage on the outward journey comes into view. Continue to the lane turning left retracing your steps to emerge at Bryn Du farm.

At this point you can turn left to return to Porth Oer, once again marvelling at the spectacular coastal scenery by taking the cliff path. An alternative is to continue on the quiet country lane back to the car park. The easier option is a stroll of just over a mile along quintessential country lanes bounded by earth and stone banks, bedecked with a profusion of wild flowers during summer, although equally colourful with their autumnal hues during the later part of the year.

At the T junction turn left passing Capel Carmel Baptist Chapel built in 1810. Continue on the lane passing Carreg farm and the disused quarry at Mynydd Carreg, now a popular view point from the small turret on top of the hill. The lane continues for a short distance before the sign post directs you left, heading seaward to find the car park.

The Welsh Black cattle are equally at home on lowland pasture or upland areas. Steeped in history they have been a valued part of rural Wales for many centuries.

Honeysuckle grows freely among the hedgerows and is a delight in full flower, its exquisite aroma filling the evening air.

LLANGWNNADL

The original site of the church of St Gwynhoedl Llangwnnadl was established here in the sixth century when early Celts arrived by sea. A bronze Sanctus bell from the site dating from the sixth century is now located in the National Museum, Cardiff with a replica taking its place. During renovation in the 1940s a stone was discovered with connection to Gwynhoedl, one of the earliest saints of Llŷn. The stone dates from the seventh century.

The original stone structure would have been a straightforward rectangle shape dating from Norman times. The church would have been the last stopping off point for the pilgrims in the Middle Ages before reaching Aberdaron ahead of the ultimate part of their passage to Bardsey. This eventful period was to witness the addition of the south aisle together with the construction of the present doorway in the south wall.

Both additional aisles were built to the same proportion as the original structure with three four-centred arches and octagonal columns providing support.

The prosperous Tudor period was to result in a programme of extending churches throughout Wales. As a result the north aisle was built in the early 1500s. The original building was renovated with a large window built into the east wall to mirror the more recent north and south aisle. Both additional aisles were built to the same proportions as the original structure, with three four-centred arches and octagonal columns providing support. 1850 was to see more renovations carried out and again in the 1960s.

The north aisle was built during the prosperous Tudor period.

The view from the east.

The decorative gate and southern doorway.

Standing stones located from OS mapping can at times be a little disappointing, no more than perhaps a rubbing stone for cattle. An exception can be found just under half a mile south of the church at Llangwnnadl at grid reference 208 325. Set on a small rise within sight of the sea the magnificent monolith stands just over 10ft high.

Llangwnnadl standing stone.

PORTH COLMON

Continue coastward from Llangwnnadl to discover the delightful small cove of Porth Colmon taking the narrow winding lanes that exhibit a colourful display from spring through to the summer, when wild flowers bedeck the hedgerows. An alternative approach to the cove can be taken at low tide from the nearby sands of Traeth Penllech. The cove and natural harbour with a small slipway is a popular location for fishermen.

The delightful small cove of Porth Colmon can be found at the end of winding lanes bedecked with a variety of wild flowers through spring until late summer.

Opposite: The rocky coastline is a quiet place to sit and observe the waves pounding the shore.

During summer the wild beauty of the quiet lanes and coastal fringes of Llŷn are adorned by swathes of the brightly coloured orange-red flowers of the Montbretia, their display enhanced, dancing in the gentlest of breezes. Originating from South Africa having a variety of eight species, Montbretia was named after the French botanist Conqebert de Montbret (1780–1801).

The botanical name 'Crocosmia' is derived from the Greek krokos and osme referring to the aroma of saffron.

Montbretia grows in any soil conditions, but thrives best in coastal locations. Although naturalised throughout Britain for gardeners, Montbretia is ideal for growing in herbaceous borders with the flowers excellent for cutting. The plant is hardy enough to survive as far north as the Hebrides. Forming dense clumps with new corms continually produced below ground, the plants soon take a firm foothold hold on their location.

The inviting track tempts you down to the sea.

PORTH YSGADEN

Situated at the end of a rough stony track, bordered by an infinite variety of wild flowers and grasses during the summer months, is the delightful natural harbour of Porth Ysgaden. The port takes its name from sgaden believed to be Welsh for herring. The port was once an important link to the outside world via Liverpool as the roads of Llŷn were no more than dirt tracks making travel over long distances very difficult. The port was the only means of trade for local people with vessels delivering essential supplies including tea, salt, limestone, iron and coal.

Thomas Pennant, the foremost 18th-century Welsh intellectual and prolific author who was best known for *A Tour in Wales*, said 'Herring were taken in abundance between Porth Ysgaden and Bardsey Island. The catch was normally valued at around £4,000. The catch was either salted ashore or taken directly to Dublin by Irish wherries'.

The first derelict building you come across is the limekiln, its top today covered by a substantial metal grill. The Limekiln was fired by coal to produce the quicklime, the process was, however, hazardous and took several days, requiring constant attention.

As you near the end of the lane the setting is enhanced by the boat which may, or may not, have been abandoned.

The kiln had a cup shaped burning chamber with the air being drawn in at the base. The limestone, when delivered, would have to be crushed by hand before being ready to load into the kiln. A layer of coal was emptied in from the top of the kiln followed by an equal layer of limestone. Subsequent layers were built up until the kiln was full. The fire was then lit with kindling wood at the base. The process would take a day or two to load the kiln, three to five days for the fire to spread upward with constant attention to rake out the ash during this time, two days to cool and a further day to rake out the burnt contents through the base. Half a tonne of coal would normally produce a tonne of quicklime. Poisonous fumes were produced from the process and it has been said that many people would have fallen asleep at the top of the chamber where it was warm (remembering they would spend a week constantly tending the fire), only to be overcome by the fumes.

The limestone once burnt became quicklime essentially for local farmers to spread on the land.

Opposite: The hedgerows of the golden stony track are a delight when in full bloom, with an infinite variety of wild flowers during the summer months, especially when set against the azure sea.

Machinery like this tractor believed to be a David Brown embraces a timeless feel in the countryside.

As you look out to sea the gable end of a cottage is all that remains, once home of the customs officer who would walk the cliffs overlooking the harbour keeping an eye out for smugglers. The cottage is believed to have been inhabited right up until 1935 by local coal merchants, until a fatal accident occurred when one of the family fell from the cliff top onto the rocks below.

Wonderful views unfold eastward along the rugged northern coast of Llŷn toward Porth Dinllaen headland continuing on to the distant peaks of Yr Eifl.

As we head east from the harbour at Porth Ysgaden another gem is still to be discovered, the secluded bay of Porth y Cychod known locally as boats cove. No vehicle access is possible to the bay, with the cliffs above the cove dotted with rustic iron sheds and rusting engines, used to power the winches, all adding to the serene timeless feeling of the quintessential fishing bay.

Opposite: The custom officer's cottage. He patrolled the cliff top overlooking the harbour and would receive a share of any goods seized from smugglers.

The gable end is all that remains of the former custom officer's cottage.

The Kiln. Limestone would be delivered to the harbour along with other essential supplies. Once turned into quicklime it would be spread onto the fields by local farmers.

113

The boats and rusting equipment of the secluded bay of Porth y Cychod, known locally as boats cove create a quintessential coastal scene.

Opposite: This well weather-proofed stone and corrugated building atop the cliff appears to harmonize with the landscape.

The secluded cove of Porth y Cychod lies to the north of Porth Ysgaden.

The vantage point of the old custom officer's cottage is clear to see.

Trig points or triangulation pillars were built to assist an accurate geographical survey of Great Britain, beginning in 1935. Mainly associated with the higher peaks, trig points were, however, built in some low lying areas, as is the case here above Porth Ysglaig, less than 50ft above sea level. The positioning of the trig points was such that at least two others could be seen from any one. By sitting a theodolite on the concealed mountings on top of the pillars, accurate bearing to the nearest trig points could be taken. This process called triangulation covered the whole country and led to the OS maps we use today. A benchmark was set on the side inscribed with the letters 'OSBM' (Ordnance Survey Bench Mark) and the reference number of the trig point.

The two nearest triangulation pillars lie 4 miles south-east on the summit of Carn Fadryn at grid reference 278 351 and 10 miles north-east on the unmistakable summit of Yr Eifl at grid reference 365 447, both destinations yet to be visited.

The standard design was attributed to Brigadier Martin Hotine then head of the trigonometrical department at Ordnance Survey. No longer used, due to the development of aerial photography and GPS, some have been removed but many remain not least as an icon of the countryside but as a valuable reference point for walkers.

The trig point stands less than 50ft above sea level, the next in line is on the summit of Yr Eifl, the summit of Llŷn clearly visible in the distance. The concealed mountings on the top of triangulation pillars were used to accommodate a theodolite to obtain an accurate reading.

Carn Fadryn is one of Llŷn's major hill forts set atop an extinct volcano overlooking the village of Garnfadryn.

CARN FADRYN

The hedgerows come alive with the promise of new growth during early spring.

Heading south-east from Porth Ysgaden to the village of Garnfadryn we are now a mere 4 miles north–west from Llanbedrog. Carn Fadryn is one of Llŷn's major hill forts set atop an extinct volcano overlooking the village. The remains of stone circles are to be found around the hillside. Carn Fadryn sits almost at the centre of the peninsula, consequently providing a 360 degree panorama from the summit. The name Carn Fadryn is believed to be associated with Madren, granddaughter of Gwrtheyrn who was said to have fled from Nant Gwrtheyrn to seek refuge here on Carn Fadryn.

Near to the summit are the remains of a castle. The castle fortifying the natural crag built during the 12th century is believed to have been the castle of the sons of Owain of Gwynedd, also known as Owen the Great, 'King of Gwynedd', from 1137 until his death in 1170. After his death, Owain Gwynedd was buried in Bangor Cathedral where his tomb can still be seen today.

After his death his sons, Dafydd and Rhodri, allegedly killed their older half brother Hywel with Gwynedd becoming divided, a situation that was to remain until Llewellyn the Great took complete control over most of Wales.

The fine example of an Iron Age Hill Fort with remains of circular buildings contained within the defensive outer walls can be seen near the summit. It seems that two periods of fort building has taken place on Carn Fadryn, the first period dates from 300BC with the summit becoming enclosed, the second phase appears to have fortified the enclosure and dates from 100BC.

To the north of the summit, a huge slab of rock with a flat surface can be found, known as King Arthur's Table. It is the site of a deep well, being partly concealed by stones. Legend has it that the waters could 'heal eye defects and was a remedy for several feminine ailments'.

Early morning dew creating intricate patterns.

The cipher on the brightly painted post box dates installation after 1953.

PORTH DINLLAEN

Porth Dinllaen, as we have discovered from the earlier part of our journey, has a story to be told of what might have been. Porth Dinllaen was originally a fishing port that grew around the natural harbour at the west end of the bay. The harbour is unique on Llŷn in that it is sheltered from the prevailing south westerly winds, facing east and is therefore only adversely affected by north-easterly winds. The shelter afforded from the headland would have been a determining factor to its development as a busy trading centre during the 19th century, a time when most provisions would have been brought by sea. It is believed that upwards of 900 ships a year passed through the port during the mid 1800s. The port had earned a reputation for being a safe haven and ships would seek shelter when storms threatened. In 1863 after severe storms the local priest wrote to the Royal National Lifeboat Institution (RNLI) to request a lifeboat be stationed at Porth Dinllaen. A boat shed complete with a slipway was constructed and has been manned ever since by volunteers.

The busy port was used for exporting as well as importing essential supplies along with salt for the herring trade at Nefyn. With pig farming an important part of agriculture on Llŷn the port was essential to export cargo to Liverpool.

Things could nevertheless have been so different for this remote village, as in May 1806, a parliamentary bill was published approving new buildings: it was thought that Porth Dinllaen would be chosen as the preferred route to Dublin rather than Holyhead on Anglesey. From 1806 the Royal mail was dispatched to Ireland from Porth Dinllaen bringing thoughts of what may follow. The Porth Dinllaen Harbour Company was formed in 1808 with plans put forward for a rail terminus. Road and pier building began which can be seen today with the lasting legacy of a straight section of road as you approach Porth Dinllaen. The hotel and a cluster of houses were built above the beach in anticipation of the vast numbers of travellers passing through. The bill was, however, rejected in 1810 in favour of Holyhead, and the rest as they say is history.

Opposite: Sunset over Porth Dinllaen: originally a fishing port that grew around the natural harbour at the west end of the bay. The harbour is unique to Llŷn, sheltered from the prevailing south westerly winds.

H Andy Boatman launching service from the beach at Porth Dinllaen.

The village remains much as it was with a cluster of cottages, a pub and, of course, the lifeboat station. Oh how it could have been so different, an exploit that may well have affected the relative tranquillity of not only the immediate surrounding area, but the whole of the Lleyn Peninsula.

The lifeboat station and slipway established in 1864 was rebuilt in 1888 on the same site. The present structure, with its extended slipway, was completed in 1925. Plans are underway to create a state of the art building suitable for the 21st century.

The bay today is a haven for pleasure craft, a far cry from the busy days of the 19th century when the bay was an important shipping centre.

A wonderful array of pebbles can be found along the more rugged north coast of Llŷn.

Opposite: From Porth Dinllaen, Yr Eifl now begins to presents a more formidable aspect in contrast to the relatively distant views afforded to the summit of Llŷn on our journey so far.

Sunset over the idyllic harbour; it is believed that upwards of 900 ships passed through the port a year during the mid 1800s.

NEFYN

Man's first recorded occupation of this delightful part of Llŷn can be traced back to the Iron Age, with the hill fort set atop Garn Boduan towering 917ft above Nefyn. The site consisted of 170 round stone huts and ramparts that are still visible today. They were almost certainly the first inhabitants of Nefyn over two thousand years ago. Documentary evidence of Nefyn can be traced back to the late 11th century with reference being made to the Welsh Prince Gruffydd ap Cynan and in 1188 to Gerald de Barri better known as Gerald of Wales, the son of a Norman Knight who undertook a journey around Wales in pre map times, accompanying the Archbishop of Canterbury as recruitment officer for a crusade in the Middle East. At Portmeirion he described his crossing the Traeth Mawr and the Traeth Bychan from where the journey continued directly across Llŷn to Nefyn. It is said that Gerald found an extremely rare manuscript at Nefyn in contrast to what had been described as a literary wilderness throughout the earlier part of his journey. Their journey continued east on horseback to Caernarfon, crossing Bwlch yr Eifl between the two most northern peaks of Yr Eifl, never visiting the remote lands end of Llŷn.

In 1284 Edward I of England celebrated his victory over the Welsh, holding a jousting tournament at Nefyn said to have been attended by knights from all over Europe.

The main influence on Nefyn's development, as would be expected, has to be the sea, playing an important role in the town economy. Fishing for herring became the principal trade from the early 1800s. A fleet of small boats would have been used to fish for the shoals of herring but the shoals, along with the fishing fleet, vanished in the late 1900s. The influence of the herring trade should not be underestimated and is commemorated on the town's coat of arms which bears three herrings. There is an exhibition housed in the Old St Mary's Church, dedicated to the maritime history of Nefyn, which is worth a visit. The site of the church dates from the sixth century with the present structure built in 1827. The church was an important stopping off point for the Pilgrims en route to Bardsey Island. Nefyn Watch Tower (Y Twr) situated atop a Norman Motte is another reminder of the past. The tower was used as a look out for the huer who would cry out when he had spotted a shoal of herring, to inform the fleet of their course. The maritime theme was sustained between 1760 and 1880, as it was throughout Llŷn, with the building of some 120 ships at Nefyn and a further 45 vessels built at Porth Dinllaen between 1776 and 1864.

Earthquakes are not readily associated with the British Isles but in July 1984 an earthquake measuring 5.4 on the Richter scale with the epicentre close to Nefyn was recorded, one of the strongest to hit the British Isles in modern times. Fortunately only minor structural damage was reported but the aftershock was said to have been widely felt across England and Wales.

Opposite: The vast sweeping sandy bay is a delight for sun seekers and sailors. The beach huts are testament to the popularity of Porth Nefyn.

The influence of the herring trade should not be underestimated, and is commemorated on the town coat of arms, bearing three herrings.

Our journey continues east, following the tracks of Gerald of Wales, leaving behind Nefyn with a spectacular coastline unfolding in the distance. Ahead, the northern slopes of Yr Eifl rise abruptly from the sea, a striking mountain mass that stands guard over, and dominates, the North Llŷn coast. The mountain mass consists of three peaks. The highest, Garn Ganol, at 1,849ft is the highest point of Llŷn, its summit the site of an ancient cairn. Garn For, the northern summit, is separated by the pass of Bwlch yr Eifl. The third summit, Tre'r Ceiri on the southern side, is the location of an Iron Age hill fort said to be one of the best surviving examples of a prehistoric hill fort in Britain.

The old St Mary's Church, Nefyn.

Opposite: There is an exhibition housed in the Old St Mary's Church, dedicated to the maritime history of Nefyn. The site of the church dates from the sixth century with the present structure built in 1827. The church was an important stopping off point for Pilgrims on their journey to Bardsey Island.

The Church of St Beuno at Pistyll on the pilgrim's route was another important stopping off point for worship on their journey to Ynys Enlli.

PISTYLL CHURCH

The Church of St Beuno at Pistyll nestles in a hollow beside a stream within touching distance of the sea. The church on the Pilgrim's route was another important stopping off point for worship on their journey to Ynys Enlli. The original structure was of wood and plaster with a thatched roof, later to be replaced by a more substantial stone building. It was not only pilgrims that made the journey to Pistyll, there was a hospice nearby where lepers came to seek a cure. A small leper's window on the north-western end of the church allowed the infected to remain outside during mass, preventing the risk of infection to the assembled congregation.

The church treasures include a 12th-century font and the remains of a mediaeval wall painting said to depict St Christopher, discovered during restoration of the church in 1949.

The tradition of celebrating Lammas was revived in 1969 when the church was decorated with sweet smelling wild medicinal herbs and rushes laid upon the floor during Christmas, Easter and August. Lammas comes from the Anglo-Saxon word 'hlaef-mas' loaf mass, when the first grains of harvest were used to bake a loaf. The loaf would have been given in celebration with a time of feasting and prayer to ensure the rest of the harvest would be safely gathered in.

Opposite: The painted board over the altar reads 'Clodforwch yr Arglwydd canys da yw' 'Praise the Lord for he is good'.

The tradition of celebrating the Lammas has been revived with the church freshly carpeted with rushes and sweet smelling wild medicinal herbs three times a year.

CLODFORWCH YR ARGLWYDD CANYS DA YW.

129

The churchyard is the last resting place of the actor Rupert Davies who appeared in many television series. His many roles included appearances in *Quatermass II* and *Dangerman*, but he was best known for playing the title role in the BBC 1960s television series *Maigret*, based on the *Maigret* novels written by Georges Simenon.

Over a century ago this delightful, peaceful spot would have been reverberating to the sounds of explosions from the granite quarries. The village population grew twentyfold with the arrival of quarrymen from all corners of Britain. A way-marked path leads across National Trust land to the cliffs above Pistyll Bay where you may be fortunate to get a sighting of the rare chough.

The land to the north-east of the church is owned by the National Trust with a right of way forming part of The Lleyn Peninsula Coastal Path.

Opposite: Over a century ago this delightful peaceful spot would have been reverberating to the sounds of explosions from the granite quarries.

The original structure of St Beuno's was later replaced by the present stone building.

Opposite: Low evening light serves to enhance the rugged north coast east of Pistyll.

As you gain height ascending the bridal path the views to the coast begin to unfold on your left down through the valley of Nant Gwrtheyrn.

YR EIFL WALK

Distance 4 miles, with an estimated time of 3–3.5 hours.

Without doubt this is one of the most challenging walks that Llŷn has to offer. Despite the modest height, the going is more akin to the loftier regions of its near neighbour Snowdonia. The reward for the effort, however, is superb, with views from the summit that encompass the whole sweep of Cardigan Bay to the south and the majestic Snowdonia range to the east. The magnificent view west along the entire Lleyn Peninsula extends to the distant Wicklow Mountains of Ireland, given the right weather conditions those same conditions can provide a glimpse of the Isle of Man to the north.

Unlike the other walks on Llŷn this one should not be underestimated. It should not be attempted in misty conditions and a good pair of walking boots is essential to tackle the rocky terrain.

The walk begins at the Forestry Commission car park just a little north of Llithfaen just off the B4417 at grid reference 353 440. On leaving the car park turn right, then in a very short distance you bear left onto a bridal way, heading progressively upward to the pass of Bwlch yr Eifl. This pass separates your first destination, the summit of Garn Ganol and the northern peak of Garn For. The views to the coast begin to unfold on your left downwards through the valley of Nant Gwrtheyrn.

The present village of Nant Gwrtheyrn was built in 1878 to house the quarrymen and their families. The village consisted of 26 houses, a mansion, shop and chapel. By the 1940s the quarry had closed, and the last residents left in 1959 allowing the whole village to fall into disrepair. Thomas Pennant had visited Nant Gwrtheyrn while writing his *Tour of Wales* in the late 18th century. He described a tumulus by the sea at the bottom of Nant Gwrtheyrn, a stone grave covered by earth, called Gwrtheyrn's Grave.

135

As you begin the final ascent to the summit of Llŷn the views open up to reveal the sheer beauty of the rugged north coast.

Legend has it that following the death of Grwtheyrn, three monks came to the original village while staying at St Beuno's Church, Clynnog fawr to convert the residents, but were thrown out by the heathen villagers. What follows is known as the curse of Nant when the monks cast three curses upon the village.

The first curse stated that Nant's ground would never be holy again and anyone who died in the village could not be buried there. Second, that no man or woman from the village would be allowed to marry one another and thirdly that the village would become deserted.

An old Welsh folk tale tells of the curse 'The Curse of Nant Gwrtheyrn'. A young couple follow the tradition of the village, that the bride must hide on the morning of the wedding and that the husband find her and escort her to the ceremony. The girl hides in a hollow tree where the sweethearts used to meet when they were courting, but her young suitor fails to find her because of the curse. Months and months pass and the young man thinks his bride-to-be has run away from him. He shelters beneath a hollow tree during a storm and a flash of lightning shoots down at the tree cracking it open and the skeleton of his sweetheart fell out before him, still in her wedding dress. He died soon afterwards of a broken heart, and the two lovers were placed in the same coffin, but even there they were not to rest in peace. As the cart carrying the coffin was climbing the hill out of the valley, it hit a rock and the coffin was shaken off and tumbled down the cliff to sink into the sea, doomed by the second curse.

The third curse appeared to have been fulfilled when the earlier decline in quarrying caused the final abandonment of the village in the late 1950s allowing the buildings to fall into a state of disrepair.

The heather clad hillside is transformed into a swathe of purple when the plant is in full bloom.

On the north-west slopes are the remains of stone settlements.

137

The upper slopes of the northern approach are strewn with large boulders, necessitating some scrambling to reach the summit trig point.

Bilberries grow wild on the upper slopes.

The Nant Grwtheyrn Trust bought the land in 1978. Having fully restored the village, it is now home to Nant Gwrtheyrn Welsh Language and Heritage Centre where the Welsh language is introduced to hundreds of students every year. The Heritage Centre opened in 2003 providing visitors to the village the opportunity to learn about the Welsh language and culture.

At the top of the pass, as the views unfold along the north cost of Llŷn, take the track heading in a southerly direction on your right, opposite the metal gate, to begin the ascent of Garn Ganol, the central and highest peak. Towards the stony summit some scrambling is required but the nature of the large slabs eases the final part of the climb. Once at the summit you are now 1,849ft above sea level, the highest point of Llŷn, with its triangulation pillar and large cairn. Your reward for the effort thus far is to be greeted with a magnificent panorama said to be one of the finest in Wales. To the east, the distant shores of Anglesey and Caernarfon Castle are visible. The majestic sweep of the Snowdonia mountain range as it runs south to the Rhinogs and Cadair Idris provides a magnificent backdrop to Cardigan Bay. It is said on a clear winter's day that the Pembrokeshire coast is visible. The view west encompasses the arm of Llŷn to Aberdaron and beyond to Bardsey Island.

The concealed mountings accommodated a theodolite to obtain accurate readings assisting the accurate geographical survey begun in 1935.

Trig points or triangulation pillars were built to assist an accurate geographical survey of Great Britain beginning in 1935. Trig points are not restricted to the loftier regions. As we saw at Porth Ysgaden, where the height of the trig point is only a few feet above sea level.

After spending some considerable time in awe of the panorama the summit affords, the route continues towards the southernmost peak of Tre'r Ceiri and its Iron Age hill fort. Continue in a more south-easterly direction between the summit and the rocky outcrop following the path as it heads down the slopes of Garn Ganol. At a fork, keep to the left path passing large boulders, heading into the valley between the two peaks. Continue over rough grassland to a path ahead, the route to the next summit. After a short climb the path goes through a gap in the remains of a stone outer wall, our first encounter with the Iron Age hill fort of Tre'r Ceiri, believed to derive from Cewri 'town of the giants' or an alternative theory suggesting Ceiri meaning castle or fortress. What is not in doubt is that once inside the outer ramparts the remains of 150 huts can be seen, some with walls over 3ft high. The huts consist of several round houses, some rectangle and some oval in shape. The huts were built in groups across the fort.

Opposite: The views from the summit complete with triangulation pillar are awe inspiring to Snowdonia eastward, and south as far as St David's Head in Pembrokeshire, visible on a clear day.

The summit towers over the southernmost peak of Tre'r Ceiri and its Iron Age hill fort. Inside the outer ramparts the remains of 150 huts can be seen some with walls over 3ft high.

A rocky outcrop near the summit provides breathtaking views.

Extensive surveys carried out during 1956 produced evidence of occupation by the Romans, earlier finds date from AD150–400. Ponder for while and it is easy to imagine what it must have been like two thousand years ago, a bustling village scene with the aroma of wood smoke rising from within the roofs of the stone huts, all set within the safe haven of the Iron Age hill fort.

The route continues by retracing your steps downward through the outer rampart wall to take the left path that descends into the valley. Continue heading in a south westerly direction, bearing slightly right until you arrive at another fork where you take the right hand path crossing a ladder stile.

Far left: Yr Wyddfa, Snowdon summit standing above a blanket of cloud rises to 3,560ft above sea level. The distance from Yr Eifl just over 16 miles north-east as the crow flies.

Left: Nature never disappoints, a visitor to the summit rests to soak up the warmth of the late summer sun.

The restored cottages of Nant Gwrtheyrn now provide accommodation for the students at The Welsh Language and Heritage Centre. The centre specialises in courses for adults who want to learn Welsh as a second language.

Continue along the path heading towards the village of Llithfaen directly in front of you. On reaching another ladder stile, continue over until you come upon a track. Immediately before the farm buildings, take the right turn north-eastwards heading directly back to the Forestry Commission car park, keeping the wall on your left. The village of Nant Grwtheyrn is well worth a visit. One option is to continue walking but it is a long hard slog back, however, it is just a short drive by car, negotiating a couple of hairpin bends on the way.

The restored village provides a chance of refreshment after the exhilarating walk across the summit of Llŷn and a visit to Nant Gwrtheyrn Heritage Centre. Nant has an aura of stillness about the valley unlike anywhere else on Llŷn making it easy to sit and contemplate what life would have been like over a century ago, when quarrying for granite was at its height. 1861 saw the opening of Port Nant quarry with an estimated 200 people living in the village. The granite sets would have been shipped to the growing cities in the North of England.

Nant has an aura of stillness about the valley unlike anywhere else on Llŷn making it easy to sit and ponder what life would have been like over a century ago. Many relics remain on display as a reminder of Nant Gwrtheyrn's rich industrial past.

143

The west tower almost certainly dates from the early 16th century.

CLYNNOG FAWR

The churchyard lies within sight of the sea.

As we leave behind the lofty peaks of Llŷn, ahead is a relatively low lying area of land barley no more than just a few feet above sea level, an area that continues the length of the coastal fringes for the remaining 10 miles before arriving at Caernarfon. No further major areas of habitation occur, with the exception of Bontnewydd, a couple of miles outside Caernarfon. From time to time you come across a small village with a substantial church centred at the heart of the community and here at Clynnog fawr that is unquestionably the case. The significant church is dedicated to St Beuno.

St Beuno was an active missionary who, under the protection of Cadfan, the King of Gwynedd in the early seventh century, founded a monastery here at Clynnog. The present building dates from the prosperous 15th and 16th century with evidence suggesting that the current chapel was built on the site of the original chapel of St Beuno.

Legend associates St Beuno with miraculous healing powers. St Beuno's well is situated close by and legend has it that patients were dipped in the waters and then lay overnight on a tombstone in the churchyard to recover.

History tells us that the church suffered at the hands of the Vikings and the Normans. The church ,due to its location and importance, was a vital stopping off point for pilgrims on their journey to Bardsey. Located inside the church is a chest hewed from a single piece of ash and is most likely to be mediaeval in origin.

The present structure stands on top of much earlier foundations laid down by St Beuno in the seventh century. St Beuno established his church at Clynnog fawr, often referred to as just Clynnog. The church was originally the site of a large clas, a cross between a monastery and a college.

CAERNARFON

The final part of our journey through Llŷn ahead of reaching Anglesey is heralded as we enter the town of Caernarfon, the northern gateway to the peninsula, located at the southern end of the Menai Strait, set between the North Wales coast and Anglesey. The castle is the dominant feature of the town and is said to be the most impressive of all the castles built by Edward I, one of the world's most iconic mediaeval fortresses.

It was, however, the Romans who first fortified Caernarfon, at the time named 'Segontium', situated on the southern outskirts of modern day Caernarfon. The Roman fortification was built on the banks of the Afon Seiont, positioned as it was to provide shelter for boats supplying Segontium. Little evidence remains as to the fate of Segontium after the Romans left during the fifth century.

During the 11th century William the Conqueror had turned his attention to Wales following the Norman conquest of England, and by 1086 it was believed that the Normans were in control of North Wales. In 1088 Hugh d'Avranches, the Earl of Chester built three castles in North Wales, one being at Caernarfon. This early structure would have consisted of a motte and bailey, with timber posts and earth banks.

The Welsh were to recapture Gwynedd in 1115 with castles coming into their possession. Records reveal that Llywelyn ap Iorwerth (Llywelyn the Great) and later his grandson, Llywelyn ap Gruffydd (Llywelyn the Last), spent time at Caernarfon.

In 1282 war broke out between England and Wales, a conflict that was to see the Welsh leader Llywelyn ap Gruffydd lose his life, with his brother Dafydd ap Gruffydd continuing the fight against the English, a fight that would in time be lost at the hands of the victorious Edward I in 1823.

Edward I began his march through Wales capturing castles at Dolwyddelan, Criccieth and Dolbadarn. Edward I soon embarked on a period of fortification of North Wales creating an 'iron ring' with castle building commencing at Harlech, Conwy and here at Caernarfon, to establish English rule.

Opposite: The original Roman fortification of Caernarfon, 'Segontium' as it was known, was built on the banks of the Afon Seiont.

Right: Today the river provides a haven for pleasure craft and working boats.

The 'iron ring' saw fortification at strategic sites around the coast, with supplies being brought in by sea to avoid the threat of attack as the north was always a strong hold of the Welsh, with supplies easily cut off en route through the mountains. At Caernarfon, Edward I's plans included a town within the walls, completely destroying the original settlement and castle, with the intention that Caernarfon would be the seat of power and a symbol of dominance by the English over the Welsh.

Work began in 1283 with the creation of a ditch followed by the building of a wooden barricade that would prevent attack from the enemy during construction. Excavation of the moat supplied stone for the walls that are 20ft deep at the foundations. By 1285 the castle and town walls had been constructed, making the site defensible at a cost of £12,000, or so it was thought.

The castle was invaded by Madog ap Llywelyn during a revolt in 1294, but control was regained by the English in 1295 who then set about completing the final sections of wall and The Kings Gate making the castle impregnable. The total building cost ran to £25,000. Although perhaps the most impressive of Edward I's castles, Caernarfon was not as defensible as Harlech or Beaumaris.

The accommodation on several floors was constructed within the impressive Eagle Tower, the first to be built during the initial phase. Additional building saw the creation of the Queens Tower, Chamberlain Tower and Black Tower. A Great Hall, a hall in the Kings Tower and chapels were all housed within the castle walls.

Caernarfon was garrisoned and endured against sieges by Owain Glydwr in 1403 and again in 1404 finally surrendering to Parliamentary forces in 1646.

Edward I had intended Caernarfon to be a seat of government and royal residence as opposed to merely a fortification. To emphasise this, Edward I ensured his son the first Prince of Wales, was born within the walls of the castle in 1294. Modern day history was made when the castle became the centre of worldwide attention as the setting for the investiture of HRH Prince Charles as Prince of Wales in 1969.

The castle dominates the town with its inimitable multilateral towers, daunting battlements and sheer scale, easily setting it apart from the rest.

THE
RIGHT HONOURABLE
DAVID LLOYD GEORGE O·M
PRIME MINISTER
M·P· CARNARVON BOROUGHS
AND CONSTABLE OF
CARNARVON CASTLE

SIR HUGH OWEN
BORN 1804   DIED 1881

ERECTED
BY
A GRATEFUL NATION

Castle Square has been the site of a weekly market dating from the late 13th century. Standing in the corner of the square is the statue of David Lloyd George, MP for Caernarvonshire and Prime Minister during World War One. Set within the square is another statue dedicated to Sir Hugh Owen, a tireless worker for the establishment of education in Wales.

To cater for the transportation of welsh slate, mined in Snowdonia during the late 1800s, Victoria Dock was built. As the slate industry began to decline the dock saw little trade and fell into disrepair. The docks have recently found a new lease of life with the creation of a yachting marina. The area known as Doc Fictoria is now a popular destination for visitors, with new hotels, restaurants and an arts centre all within just a short distance from Caernarfon Castle, and complemented with views across the Menai Strait to our next destination, Anglesey.

The coast of Anglesey is less than a mile across the tidal Menai Strait.

Regenerated, Doc Fictoria is now a popular destination for visitors to Caernarfon.

Victoria Dock was built in the 1870s to provide harbour facilities to cater for the export of slate from Caernarfon. Today Doc Fictoria's harbour side marina has been transformed providing moorings for luxury craft, cafés and restaurants and a maritime museum alongside shops and hotels.

Edward I had intended Caernarfon to be a seat of government and royal residence, as opposed to merely a fortification.

Below the castle walls is the terminus of The Welsh Highland Railway. A narrow gauge, steam hauled train service now departs from Caernarfon taking a scenic journey for 25 miles, first climbing to the foothills of Snowdonia before passing through the picturesque village of Beddgelert. Several stations allow passengers to explore Snowdonia with ease. The track then continues through the Pass of Aberglaslyn descending in a series of twists and turns to reach the regained Glaslyn estuary before arriving at Porthmadog. The line was officially opened on 12 April 2011, now allowing onward travel from Porthmadog through to Blaenau Ffestiniog – by far the longest heritage railway journey in the UK.

Her Majesty the Queen and HRH Prince Philip visited the area in 1964 and returned, travelling on The Welsh Highland Railway on the 27 April 2010.

THOMAS TELFORD'S MENAI SUSPENSION BRIDGE

It is likely that a community has existed at Menai Bridge since Roman occupation, as this provides the shortest crossing of the Menai Strait between the mainland and Ynys Mon. Prior to the construction of the bridge in 1826 a ferry connected Anglesey to the mainland with an alternative method to cross on foot available at extremely low tides. Agriculture was the main source of income for Anglesey, and the sale of cattle would necessitate a crossing of the strait, to join the drover trail to the markets of Wales, and even as far as London. The cattle would be driven across and had to swim the 200 yards to reach the safety of the mainland.

The act of union in 1800 effectively united the Kingdom of Great Britain and Ireland. As a consequence of the act the Union Flag was created commemorating the union in 1801 and still remains today. Called the Union Flag, or more popularly known as the Union Jack, it combined the flags of England and Wales, Scotland and a St Patrick's cross to represent Ireland. More importantly, the act increased the need for transport links to Dublin in Ireland with Holyhead chosen to be one of the main ports in 1810, winning the vote from Parliament ahead of Porth Dinllaen on the Lleyn Peninsula.

Thomas Telford was assigned to improve the route from London to Holyhead and his remit included building a bridge across the Menai Strait. Work began on construction of the bridge in 1819 but the design had to allow for naval ships to be given uninterrupted passage through the straits with their masts, at that time, as tall as 100ft. To meet these requirements Telford built hollow limestone towers on either side which were completed in 1824, then the bridge was suspended on 16 huge chain cables to support the 577ft length of road, between the two towers. The monumental task was completed in 1826 along with the other road improvements, with the journey time from London to Holyhead reduced from 36 to 26 hours.

The weather in perfect mood contrasting the distant Lleyn Peninsula against the bright sunshine at Llanddwyn Bay.

NEWBOROUGH WARREN and LLANDDWYN ISLAND

Edward I evicted the townsfolk of Llanfaes to make way for the building of Beaumaris Castle and resettled them in Newborough, a prosperous town surrounded by extremely fertile farmland, an area that became known as the garden of Wales. During the 13th century a series of violent storms buried the farmland under a huge blanket of sand, creating the dunes that remain today. To prevent further progress of the dunes, Queen Elizabeth I passed a law that forbid the removal of Marram Grass therefore helping to stabilise the dunes. The passing of the law not only halted the progress of the dunes it also provided a raw material for a new industry to spring up, with the grass used in the production of mats.

The Warren covers a staggering 1,585 acres and is today a popular nature reserve surrounded by beaches with the main two being Llanddwyn Bay and Malltraeth Bay. These are divided by Llanddwyn Island, a rocky outcrop formed during the Cambrian period over 570 million years ago when much of Wales lay under water. Red hot lava flowed from beneath the ocean cooling rapidly, forming the pillow lava that can be seen at the landward side of the island. The Island does remain attached to the mainland except during the highest of tides. The area has a combination of forest and open dune land with a freshwater lake, salt marsh and mud flats, the latter being important wintering grounds for waders and wildfowl. As would be expected, the reserve contains a tremendous diversification of flora including dune helleborine, butterwort and a thriving invertebrate population

The area is a combination of forest and open dune land.

158

Llanddwyn Island remains attached to the mainland except during the highest of tides.

The name Newborough Warren was derived from the vast amount of rabbits that soon colonised the dunes, although this did provide the residents with a valuable commodity with estimates of over 100,000 rabbits taken a year. The devastating epidemic of Myxomatosis during the 1950s allowed the vegetation of the dunes to take a firm hold.

Llanddwyn is derived from 'The Church of Dwynwen'. St Dwynwen is the Welsh patron saint of lovers and is celebrated, not unlike St Valentine, on 25 January. Dwynwen who is believed to be the daughter of King Brycheiniog lived during the fifth century. One legend tells that she fell in love with a young man named Maelon but her father refuses their marriage and she prays to forget her love for him. Maelon drinks a potion that an angel had prepared for Dwynwen while she was asleep, and he turns to ice. She then prays to be granted three wishes. The first that Maelon be released, the second that all true lovers find happiness and thirdly that she should never again wish to be married. Dwynwen then retreats to Llanddwyn Island to become a hermit until her death.

After her death she became the patron saint of lovers and pilgrimages were made to her holy well on the island. Legend has it that a sacred fish swims within, whose movements predict the future fortunes and relationships of various couples. Lovers who visit the well believe that if the water boils while they are present, then love and good luck will surely follow.

During the 16th century a chapel was built partly funded from the many offerings left at her shrine on the site of Dwynwen's original chapel. The ruins of the chapel can still be seen today.

The prevailing atmospheric conditions create a haze of saltwater spray, restricting the visibility of the original lighthouse on Llanddwyn Island, seen from Llanddwyn beach across a turbulent sea.

The estuary of the Afon Ffraw offers a safe anchorage for small fishing boats.

ABERFFRAW

Aberffraw borders the estuary of the Afon Ffraw and offers a safe harbour for small fishing boats. An ancient packhorse bridge leads to a wide expanse of sand dunes that culminate in a stretch of golden sand on Anglesey's west coast. The old village square has a chapel, pub and village shop. Today Aberffraw is a seaside village but during the early mediaeval period it was, at times, the seat of the rulers of Wales and home to the Royal family of Gwynedd. After Norman incursions into Wales, Aberffraw replaced Deganwy as the Court of the Kingdom of Gwynedd. Very little remains but a heritage centre keeps the past alive at a time when North Wales was ruled by Llywelyn ap Iorwerth (Llywelyn the Great) who was also recognised as the ruler of Wales.

East of Aberffraw can be found Llangadwaladr Church, a 12th-century structure said to have been built on the site of the burial ground of the Kings of Gwynedd. To the west the church of St Cwyfan's can be found, often referred to as the church in the sea, located as it is on a small tidal island called Cribinau situated on the west coast.

Prevailing westerly winds have formed the large sand dunes on the southern side of the village.

The old bridge that spans the Afon Ffraw was built in 1731, used only for pedestrian and cycles today. A new bridge was built in the village in 1932. Today the Aber Ffraw is narrow but this was not always the case. Over the centuries prevailing westerly winds have formed the large sand dunes on the southern side of the village, the development believed to have begun in the 13th century. During the time of the Prince of Wales being in residence in Aberffraw, the estuary would have been considerably wider and deeper making it navigable for the ships of the day.

ABERFFRAW TO St CWYFAN'S WALK

Distance 4.5 miles with an estimated time of 2.5 to 3 hours.

The walk begins at the coastal village of Aberffraw on Anglesey's west coast at grid reference 357 690. Cross the hump back bridge traversing the Afon Ffraw. Follow the track as it wends its way between the cottages before continuing close to the river bank. Remain on the track heading all the while for the headland where, in just over a mile, you leave the estuary behind, veering right to take the path above the rocky shoreline. Now head towards Braich-lwyd, all the while following the coastal path until reaching the headland. The path now continues bearing right heading for the two beaches just over half a mile north from here. Once at the first beach, continue across the bay to the causeway with the church now standing proudly on its own island. Care is needed, as the sea can cover the causeway at high tide, so please check tide times before venturing out on this walk if you intend to visit the island. Only a handful of services are now held in the church and arrangements have to be made beforehand should you want to enter the church building. The island is a perfect place for peace and solitude.

St Cwyfan's Church is often referred to as the church in the sea, located as it is on a small tidal island called Cribinau situated on the west coast of Anglesey close to the estuary village of Aberffraw. The church can be reached at low tide. When built in the seventh century the church was part of the mainland, but due to coastal erosion of the boulder clay cliffs, it is now separated from the mainland, standing as it does on its own tidal island, completely cut off at high tide. The original site of Cwyfan's, also known as Llangwyfan, was founded during the seventh century with the original construction consisting of wattle and daub, usually a mixture of wet clay and straw. The present structure is said to date from the 12th century, a period when most churches throughout Britain were constructed in their present form. Much restoration work would have been carried out during the 14th century with the present roof timbers said to date from the 16th century. The church fell into disrepair during the late 1800s. Restoration took place, with the massive sea walls built that you see today, giving the island its characteristic shape. Today the exterior of the building is finished in traditional lime wash, part of a grant given by CADW, the historic environment service of the Welsh Assembly Government. CADW pronounced cad-oo is Welsh meaning to keep. An organ was donated to the church in 2008 but had to be carried across the causeway by the church wardens and local volunteers.

A row of colourful cottages front the estuary on its northern bank.

When built in the seventh century St Cwyfan's Church was part of the mainland but due to coastal erosion of the boulder clay cliffs it is now separated from the mainland standing on its own tidal island.

To return to Aberffraw, cross Porth Cwyfan sands to join a quiet country lane that meanders for a mile and half before reaching the old packhorse bridge and the start point. The lane is a delight to walk, bedecked with wild flowers during summer months and plentiful supplies of natures harvest should you visit during the autumn. You may well wish to retrace your steps, returning by the outward route with views inland of the estuary and Aberffraw unfolding, views that you may have missed on the outward journey.

The Royal Air Force maintains a 24-hour search and rescue service covering the whole of the United Kingdom and a large surrounding area.

RAF VALLEY

RAF Valley dates back to February 1941, originally named RAF Rhosneigr after the village located just south of the station. The name change to RAF Valley came barely a few weeks after opening on 5 April 1941.

March 1941 witnessed the first squadron to the base, No 305 Squadron who moved from Speke with its Hurricanes and flew convoy patrols over the Irish Sea. No 615 Squadron replaced No 305 in May 1941 and was later joined by No 219 Squadron. June 1941 saw the formation of No 456 Squadron (Royal Australian Air Force). The squadron remained at RAF Valley until March 1943 during which time they had accounted for the destruction of four enemy aircraft.

During August 1941 RAF Valley assumed responsibility for two air-sea rescue launches based close to the airfield at Rhoscolyn Bay, yet delivery was not taken until November that year. Three months earlier a tragic accident occurred, an aircraft force-landed in rough sea off Rhosneigr beach. The crew of the Botha sadly drowned along with 11 other people including airman from RAF Valley who attempted in vain to rescue the drowned crew. The incident was witnessed by two young boys from Rhosneigr who courageously put to sea in a sailing dingy in an effort to reach the downed aircraft. Despite their heroic efforts, they too were capsized by mountainous seas. Spectators on the beach roped themselves together and waded out to rescue the two boys who would subsequently be awarded The George Cross for their bravery by the King.

October 1941 saw the formation of No 275 Squadron at the station for air-sea rescue duties. At its peak over 500 officers and airwomen were stationed at the base. By 1943 enemy aircraft activity over the Irish Sea had diminished to the extent that the base was considered for a terminal for Trans Atlantic flights by American aircraft for delivery to the Royal Air Force to bolster the United States Air Force Squadrons based in England. For the remainder of the war the station would become the centre for receiving aircraft from the United States and Canada for onward dispatch to war bases throughout Britain.

May 1945 saw the United States transporting its aircraft from Britain to the Far East where the war against Japan continued. With the aircraft all departed by September that year, the stations activities were reduced, providing practical training for pilots.

Valley's role was further reduced in December 1945 to provide night flying facilities for units based at more congested stations. July 1946 saw the base transferred to the control of Flying Training Command on a care and maintenance basis. April 1948 saw control passed to No 12 Group Fighter Command putting at an end the uncertainty surrounding the base with RAF Valley now becoming a permanent Royal Air Force Station. The station remained in care and maintenance status with limited facilities, however, the Mountain Rescue Team continued to turn out for stranded climbers in the Welsh Hills.

The high visibility yellow craft is manned by four operational crew members.

During the period of inactivity, a number of improvements were made to the Station. Barrack blocks were built to a new design providing a single room for each airman, a new dining hall and a considerable number of married quarters, and since 1951 it has been one of Flying Training Command's principal stations.

No 202 Advanced Flying School formed at Valley in 1951, the first unit to take up residency at the refurbished station. The purpose of the school was to provide experience flying jet aircraft for recently trained pilots. During the mid 1950s as part of reorganisation within the Royal Air Force the unit was renumbered No 7 Flying Training School and continued its previous role of training Naval pilots to fly jet aircraft.

Since becoming a flying training school, there had always been an Army Rescue launch on standby duty at Menai, 1955 saw the task taken over by the arrival of Her Majesty's Air Force Marine Craft Unit at Holyhead. The launches were later to be assisted during rescue missions by the air-sea rescue role. Initially using Sycamore helicopters these were replaced by Whirlwinds until 1976 when they were subsequently replaced by Wessex HAR2s. Since its formation in 1955 the flight had flown over 2,000 rescue missions and during 1980 alone rescued 93 people during 137 operations.

The Mountain Rescue Team was originally formed at RAF Llandwrog in August 1943 and during its first year of existence received over 400 call-outs. It was one of six similar teams throughout the UK whose proper purpose was the rescue of aircrew who had crashed or abandoned their aircraft in mountainous areas. However, it was much more frequently called out to assist climbers of all types who got into difficulties in Snowdonia or on sea cliffs and therefore worked closely with Valley's Search and Rescue (SAR) Wessex.

Today RAF Valley operates the Sea King Mark 3 aircraft in the Search and Rescue (SAR) role. Developed by Westland from the American Sikorsky S-61, the first of 15 RAF dedicated SAR aircraft entered service in September 1977. For the next 15 years Sea King and Wessex helicopters shared search and rescue duties.

The Sea Kings maximum speed of 143mph at sea level is provided by two Rolls-Royce H1400-1 Gnome turbo shafts of 1,660shp. The helicopter is just under 56ft in length with its rotor diameter being some 62ft and accommodates a crew of four with provision for a further 19 passengers.

The high visibility yellow craft is manned by four operational crew members; the captain who is in overall command of the aircraft and the flying pilot during rescue operations; the co-pilot who aids the captain with navigation, fuel planning and radios; the radar operator/winch operator whose responsibility is to voice marshal the aircraft into position and operate the radar allowing the aircraft to descend as close as possible to vessels in distress particularly in poor weather; and the winchman/paramedic who is deployed to assist casualties from the onboard hoist. His extended paramedic skills provide treatment for the casualty en-route to hospital. As a crewman the winchman also assists the pilots with navigation, performance information and lookout.

The Royal Air Force maintains a 24-hour search and rescue service covering the whole of the United Kingdom and a large surrounding area. While the service exists primarily to assist military aircrew and other personnel in distress, the vast majority of 'scrambles' are to assist civilians who find themselves in difficulties, either on land or at sea.

RAF Sea King helicopters of 22 and 202 Squadrons operate from six UK locations. Further helicopters provide SAR cover from two Royal Navy and four Maritime and Coastguard Agency contract-operated bases, giving a total of 12 helicopter units around the UK. RAF Mountain Rescue Teams (MRTs) are based at four locations in mainland Britain, each staffed by a core of eight permanent staff members and supported by 28 part-time volunteers. The Aeronautical Rescue Coordination Centre at RAF Kinloss can call upon a variety of fixed wing aircraft to assist with long range rescues.

The winchman/paramedic is deployed to assist casualties from the onboard hoist.

The arrival of the Hawk TMk2 was the first major introduction of a new aircraft at RAF Valley since the Hawk TMk1 in 1977.

ZK032

169

The RAF Valley Station Badge depicts a Dragon Rampant holding a Portcullis.

For many years RAF Valley took pride in being a Master Diversion Airfield and remained open 24 hours a day to receive aircraft either in difficulty or diverted from other bases because of bad weather. The Station adopted the heraldic devices on the badge as an indication of both its location in Wales and its task of holding the entrance to the airfield open.

The motto 'In Adversis Perfugium' translates as 'Refuge in Adversity' and originates from the years of World War Two when the Station was a welcome landing ground for aircraft operating on combat missions and patrols over the Atlantic Ocean.

Today the primary function of RAF Valley is the training of future fast-jet aircrew. No 4 Flying Training School is the largest unit based at RAF Valley and operates the Hawk TMk1 aircraft. In the current RAF training programme, the Hawk TMk1 is the first jet aircraft that a student pilot will fly. An advanced, and very successful trainer, the Hawk TMk1, is used to teach operational tactics, air-to-air and air-to-ground firing, air combat and low-level operating procedures.

With the arrival of the Hawk TMk2, the first major introduction of a new aircraft at RAF Valley since the Hawk TMk1 in 1977, the Station is entering a new and exciting period in its long association with advanced flying training. The new aircraft is the first tangible aspect of the multi-billion pound Military Flying Training System (MFTS) which is being introduced throughout the UK Armed Forces.

The Hawk Display Team is the public face of No 4 Flying Training School (4FTS) based at RAF Valley. The Display Team exists to demonstrate the professional excellence of the RAF and promote recruitment to the RAF. Evidence shows that RAF displays have inspired a significant number of people to join the RAF, as both officers and airmen, and to all trades, not just aircrew.

RAF Valley is vital to the future of the RAF, both in terms of providing new crews to front line aircraft and the facilities and services provided in many diverse areas. The Station's roles continue to mature and RAF Valley looks forward to maintaining a high profile in delivering a quality product.

RAF Valley Display Jet 2011.

The Hawk Display Team is the public face of No 4 Flying Training School (4FTS) based at RAF Valley.

A little north of Aberffraw, ahead of reaching South Stack lighthouse the road skirts the shore providing distant views across Rhosneigr to Holy Island and Anglesey's highest point, Holyhead Mountain. In the grand scheme of things mountainous it is somewhat overshadowed by its neighbours on the mainland, rising to just over 700ft above sea level.

SOUTH STACK LIGHTHOUSE

A lighthouse was first considered on this spot as far back as 1665 although it would be almost another century and a half before the first structure appeared. The first light cost £12,000 to build and was designed by the architect Daniel Alexander who was responsible for several other lighthouses and public buildings including Dartmoor prison in Devon. He was appointed as a surveyor for Trinity House while he was working for the London Dock Company. South Stack was his first lighthouse, built in 1809. Two years later he designed Farne lighthouse in Northumberland. More followed culminating with the lighthouse on Lundy Island in the Bristol Channel.

South Stack or Ynys Lawd can be found on the north-west coast of Anglesey separated from Holy Island by a 30 metre stretch of turbulent sea. The large granite cliffs form a sheer rise from the sea to reach a height of almost 200ft. The gaping chasm between Holy Island and South Stack was first bridged in 1828 by an iron suspension bridge. This structure was replaced by an aluminium bridge in 1964 with the present day footbridge completed in 1977. Prior to the first bridge the only means of crossing the deep water channel to the island was in a basket which was suspended on a hemp cable. The bridge is approached from the main land by descending 400 steps cut into the cliff face.

1909 saw the first form of incandescent light installed. Electricity was first used to power the light in 1938. The keepers were withdrawn in 1984 with the lighthouse becoming automated and remotely controlled from Trinity House in Essex.

Since its completion in 1809 the lighthouse has allowed safe passage for ships on the treacherous Dublin to Holyhead and Liverpool crossing.

The height of the tower is 92ft with the light set 198ft above the Mean High Water. The lamp intensity is 1,370,000 candela and its character is a white flash every 10 seconds. The light can be seen for 20 nautical miles with a fog horn range of two nautical miles identified with a one second blast every 30 seconds.

South Stack cliffs offer a wealth of bird life with a great vantage point from the RSPB reserve. As many as 4,000 birds visit these cliffs every year including the rare chough, guillemot, razorbill and puffin.

The large granite cliffs rise sheer from the sea to reach almost 200ft.

The height of the tower is 92ft with its light set 198ft above Mean High Water, the light flashes every 10 seconds.

LLYNNON MILL

Leaving behind Holy Island we head north-east to the village of Llanddeusant to discover an iconic Anglesey windmill. Naturally exposed to westerly winds Anglesey was an ideal location for mills to grind corn, powered by wind rather than water. In its heyday, some 50 wind and water mills were in operation, giving Anglesey the title of the 'Granary of Wales', producing more grain than any other part of Wales.

The wind powered machinery was used to grind corn, oats and barley with mill stones quarried close to Penmon on the eastern shores of Anglesey.

The early windmills on Anglesey probably date back to Roman occupation, with records showing, that in 1352 up to 60 mills were in operation. During the 1800s the island had over one hundred mills, with half of that number powered by wind. Of the remaining mills today, including some ruins almost lost to the elements, the earliest dates from the mid 1700s, with the latest completed in 1862. Anglesey was very fertile and boasted that it could feed the entire population of Wales, earning its title as Môn Mam Cymru, the Mother of Wales.

In 1815 corn laws were introduced to put in place barriers to protect cereal prices, for the producers in Great Britain and Ireland, from competition from less expensive, foreign imported cereal. The act was known as The Importation Act 1815, and continued until the act was repealed in 1846. The House of Commons had recommended that foreign grown corn was excluded, until the price of home grown corn reached £4 per quarter.

The effect of this meant that grain prices increased, and more grain needed to be grown, at a time when the population of Anglesey was also rising, creating a boom time for milling. With the act repealed by the late 19th century, mounting imports of foreign grain had reduced the amount required locally, with many farmers changing from arable to rearing cattle and pigs. Some mills continued to carry on producing small quantities of flour, with the last mill closing in 1936.

Restoration began after the council purchased the site for £10,000 in 1978. The machinery and millstones were first removed to be refurbished while the structure was repaired with the mill officially re-opening in 1984.

174

Llynnon Mill is the only working windmill in Wales.

Some mills have thankfully been restored, now used as mere dwellings, but Llynnon Mill operates as an agricultural museum, and produces stone-ground wholemeal flour.

Llynnon Mill dates back to 1775, with many of the original documents of the day preserved, revealing that the total cost of construction and furnishing was £529. The first miller was Thomas Jones, with the mill remaining in the family, passed down through the generations. A violent storm in 1918 damaged the cap, the rotating upper section, preventing it from turning to face the wind. It operated for a time when the winds were south-westerly, but eventually closed, falling into disrepair and described as dilapidated by the early 1940s. Further damage was caused in 1954 when a severe storm blew off the cap.

Restoration began after the council purchased the site for £10,000 in 1978. The machinery and millstones were first removed to be refurbished, while the structure was repaired. The mill officially reopened in 1984, fully restored and now the only working windmill in Wales, Llynnon Mill has become a symbol of Anglesey. Today the mill is a popular tourist attraction, complete with a tea room and shop, where you can buy wholemeal flour ground by the mill. A tour of the mill provides a fascinating insight to how it operates.

The beautiful east coast of Anglesey now awaits us, where we learn of a tale of tragedy at sea, an event that would bring about a service that sailors and coastal visitors today take for granted. Moelfre, lies some 12 miles due east, with our journey skirting the shore of Llyn Alaw reservoir.

Created in 1966, on marshland, Llyn Alaw is a man made reservoir, used to supply drinking water to the north half of Anglesey. Very few rivers feed the reservoir, relying as it does on winter rainfall to keep the levels up. The reservoir is just over 2.5 miles long but has a maximum depth of only 17ft. Popular with anglers, it has been known to produce wild Brown Trout up to four pounds in weight. During winter the reservoir is home to many species of wintering wildfowl.

MOELFRE

Moelfre has a small sheltered bay with fishing boats anchored on the beach and evidence of fishing to the fore.

An archetypical small fishing boat anchored on the shingle beach.

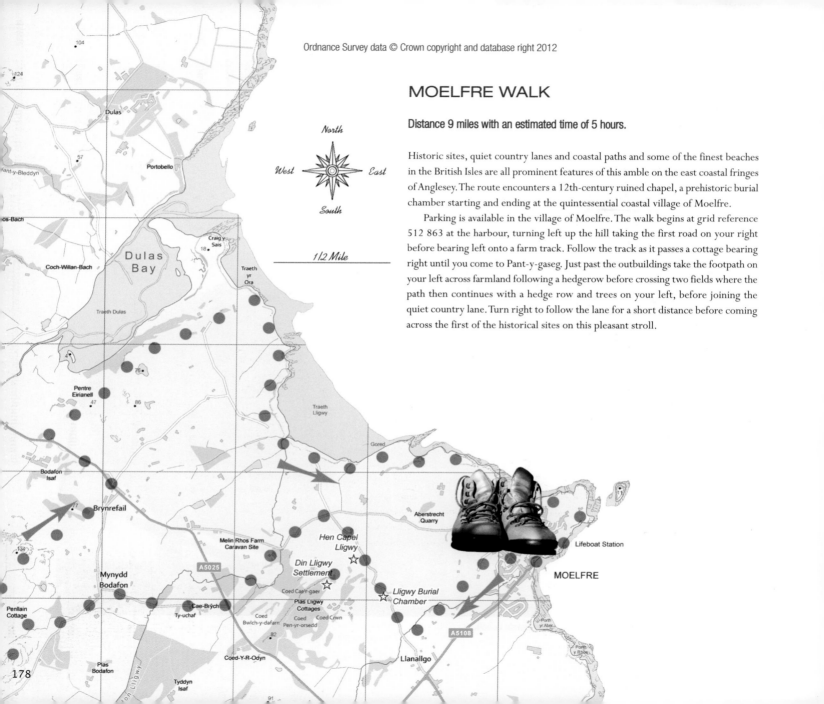

MOELFRE WALK

Distance 9 miles with an estimated time of 5 hours.

Historic sites, quiet country lanes and coastal paths and some of the finest beaches in the British Isles are all prominent features of this amble on the east coastal fringes of Anglesey. The route encounters a 12th-century ruined chapel, a prehistoric burial chamber starting and ending at the quintessential coastal village of Moelfre.

Parking is available in the village of Moelfre. The walk begins at grid reference 512 863 at the harbour, turning left up the hill taking the first road on your right before bearing left onto a farm track. Follow the track as it passes a cottage bearing right until you come to Pant-y-gaseg. Just past the outbuildings take the footpath on your left across farmland following a hedgerow before crossing two fields where the path then continues with a hedge row and trees on your left, before joining the quiet country lane. Turn right to follow the lane for a short distance before coming across the first of the historical sites on this pleasant stroll.

A magnificent bronze memorial sculpture celebrates the achievements of Moelfre's famous lifeboat-men, representing the bravery, sense of duty and purpose of all lifeboat crews.

Moelfre is a picturesque former fishing village with a long maritime history.

A kissing gate on your left leads to Lligwy Cromlech (Burial Chamber) dating from 2500–2000BC. A large stone covers the chamber and has been estimated to weigh 25 tonnes. The site was excavated in the early 1900s and revealed two separate burial groups. Rejoin the lane to continue forward with magnificent views opening on your right to reveal the majestic mountains of Snowdonia.

In a short distance a second kissing gate signed Din Lligwy and Hen Capel on your left leads down some steps where you follow the hedgerow ahead of a sign for Din Lligwy. Continue into the next field passing two metal gates, climbing some steps in the woodland to reach the enclosure and the remains of Din Lligwy. Excavations in 1905–07 produced evidence of Roman pottery dating from the fourth century. Tools and a musical instrument made from animal bones were discovered. Evidence uncovered suggested that iron working and perhaps smelting were one of the main economic activities. Despite the mainly Roman finds, the origins of the settlement may well go back into the Iron Age where it would probably have been a farming community. The excavations suggest the round structures would have been houses with the rectangular ones used for barns. Hen Capel Lligwy is a ruined 12th-century chapel built within a circular enclosure and can be found by retracing your steps following the signs. The site affords stunning views across Lligwy Bay.

Hen Capel Lligwy is a ruined 12th-century chapel built within a circular enclosure set within sight of the sea.

Lligwy Cromlech Burial Chamber dating from 2500–2000BC, the large stone covering the chamber has been estimated to weigh 25 tonnes.

Rejoin the lane and continue in the same direction until it drops down to the crossroads. Take the lane on your left for approximately a quarter of a mile, crossing a stream, then follow the sign for Rynys caravan site taking the drive through the gates passing a cottage where a path on your right leads through the caravan park. Continue on, crossing another stream taking the left track up through woodland. The path continues across open heath land before joining a defined track that leads to the road. Take the narrow lane opposite for just over half a mile arriving at a T junction. Bear left on the road for a short distance then at the right hand bend take time to visit the church of St Michael's Penrhoslligwy.

Dedicated to St Michael, it dates from the 14th century and was restored in 1865. The circular Celtic-style churchyard has many graves of the casualties from the shipwreck of the *Royal Charter* that sank off the coast at Moelfre on 26 October 1859 with the tragic loss of 454 passengers and crew.

The 2,700 tonne steamer and sailing ship bound for Liverpool ran into a severe storm in Moelfre Bay. The ships' passengers were returning from Australia many laden with gold from the Australian mines. The captain took shelter off the coast of Moelfre but the seas were so formidable, breaking the anchor chain and driving the *Royal Charter* onto the rocks breaking it in half. The passengers tried to swim ashore but to no avail, many heavily laden with their gold. Charles Dickens later made reference to the Reverend Stephen Roose who he said 'had striven tirelessly to identify and bury the dead and inform and comfort the relatives'.

The disaster had far reaching consequences, one being the Meteorological Office introducing the first gale warnings to prevent similar tragedies.

This relatively short steep section of the walk now begins with a steady climb as the lane continues uphill before a track on your right at the top of the rise. Once on the track take one of the paths on your left climbing through the heather clad hillside to reach the relatively modest summit of Yr-Arwydd complete with its triangulation pillar 584ft above sea level. The upland area is also known as Mynydd Bodafon. The views afforded from the modest summit take in the whole of Anglesey, back to the Lleyn Peninsula and across to the mountains of Snowdonia, often seen sporting their winter coats between November and March.

From the summit head back to the track in the direction of the farm at Tyn y Mynydd where you go through a metal gate to continue past a house crossing a stone stile to reach another stile. The route is way marked with yellow posts. Follow the path for just under a mile descending all the while to emerge on the roadside. Turn left passing the chapel to reach the hamlet of Brynrefail. In a short distance you reach the Pilot Boat Inn, a good place to stop and refresh having completed just over five miles of the walk.

A sculpture dedicated to the *Royal Charter* that sank off the coast at Moelfre on 26 October 1859 with the tragic loss of 454 passengers and crew is set within sight of the sea close to the lifeboat station.

The expanse of sand at Traeth Lligwy.

Once you are amply refreshed take the kissing gate to follow the path towards the sea. Magnificent coastal views are now your constant companion for much of the remainder of this delightful stroll, now following the Anglesey coastal path. Set out below on your left is the expanse of the inlet of Traeth Dulas. Ladder stiles are provided on the path and after crossing several you will emerge onto a grassy headland where outcrops of rock and patches of gorse are a delight when in full flower.

Go through a kissing gate beside a cottage to emerge onto a small lane. Follow the lane for a very short distance before bearing right onto a narrow track bordered by hedgerows where the track will emerge above the idyllic Traeth yr Ora.

Follow the cliff path as it heads toward Moelfre with the distant mass of Snowdonia dominating the views ahead. The well marked route back crosses an expanse of sand at Traeth Lligwy. At this point the ruined Hen Capel Lligwy is less than half a mile inland. The path continues around the headland passing the coastguard station and the lifeboat station ahead of reaching the harbour at Moelfre where a well deserved rest and refreshments can be taken at one of the village's pubs, cafés or restaurants.

The station's *Robert and Violet* is a Tyne class lifeboat, the first 'fast' slipway lifeboat. The last Tyne was built in 1990 and the class will be gradually replaced by the Tamar class.

ROYAL NATIONAL LIFEBOAT INSTITUTION **RNLI**

The institution was founded as a charity in 1824, later to be renamed the RNLI in 1854.

Sir William Hillary is credited with founding the National Institution, for the preservation of life from shipwreck. From his home on the Isle of Man, he saw firsthand the tragic loss of life from dozens of shipwrecks, becoming involved in many rescue attempts.

An exceptionally high standard of service has been established by generations of Moelfre lifeboat-men for which everyone in the area can be truly proud.

Sir William appealed to the Navy and the government for help in forming a national institute for the preservation of lives and property from shipwreck and with the support of London MP Thomas Wilson, and the West Indian Merchants Chairman George Hibbert, the institution was formed.

During the early 19th century, it was estimated that 1,800 ships were wrecked around the coasts of Britain every year. Coastal communities would watch helplessly as ships became stranded and broke up. Records do show that in 1730 there was a rescue boat in Liverpool, and in 1785 in Bamburgh, Northumberland, the first purpose built lifeboat was patented, by Lionel Lukin. Within 20 years, upward of 30 boats had been built and they were saving lives around the coast of Britain.

Rowing boats were initially used by the institution with the introduction of sailing boats during the 1850s. Six steam powered craft were added to the fleet during the 1890s before their development was abandoned, in favour of petrol during the early 1900s.

The first motor driven lifeboat was introduced as early as 1905, but could prove unreliable so sail rigging was still required.

The iconic inflatable was introduced in 1963 to deal with rescues inshore. 1972 saw the first B Class rigid inflatable boats, with today's B and D class lifeboats being direct descendants, now making up the bulk of the RNLI fleet.

Larger all-weather lifeboats were being developed, with each new incarnation faster and safer than its predecessor. There are now five classes of all-weather lifeboat in the RNLI fleet, with a variety of sizes, draughts and launch and recovery methods, suitable for all areas of the British and Irish coastlines.

For the RNLI's first 100 years, lifeboats were mostly launched and recovered from their local beaches. Hauling the lifeboat during launch and recovery was done by women, as most of the men were onboard. Often, farmers loaned their horses to help bear the weight.

Most large, all-weather lifeboats are designed to be launched from a slipway, or to lie afloat. Beach launches are still common, particularly with the smaller, inshore lifeboats with specially adapted tractors, to do the hauling.

MOELFRE LIFEBOAT STATION

The first station was established in the 1830s, with the first slipway constructed in 1893. The current boathouse and slipway was completed in 1909. The stations first motor lifeboat was placed on service during 1930, with Moelfre gaining its first inshore motor lifeboat in 1965.

In 1927 gold medals were awarded to Second Coxswain William Roberts and Crew Member Captain Owen Jones, and 13 bronze medals were awarded for a service in the great gales of October 1927 to the ketch *Excel*. The lifeboat had to sail right over the wreck to haul the three crew on board. The lifeboat was badly damaged and full of water, although her air-cases kept her afloat. Two men, including Crew Member William Roberts, died on board. With the Second Coxswain left completely blind for several hours, after landing, from the wind and salt water.

1959 saw a gold medal awarded to Coxswain Richard Evans, silver medal to Motor Mechanic Evan Owens and bronze medals to Second Coxswain Donald Francis and Crew Members Hugh Owen and Hugh Jones, for a service

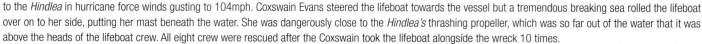

to the *Hindlea* in hurricane force winds gusting to 104mph. Coxswain Evans steered the lifeboat towards the vessel but a tremendous breaking sea rolled the lifeboat over on to her side, putting her mast beneath the water. She was dangerously close to the *Hindlea's* thrashing propeller, which was so far out of the water that it was above the heads of the lifeboat crew. All eight crew were rescued after the Coxswain took the lifeboat alongside the wreck 10 times.

In 1961 Her Majesty The Queen awarded each of the five members of the crew who took part in the *Hindlea* service with a Silver Sea Gallantry Medal. The investiture took place at Buckingham Palace on 13 July.

Coxswain Richard 'Dic' Evans was to receive a second gold medal in 1967 with a silver medal awarded to Motor Mechanic Evan Owens, and bronze medals to Second Coxswain Donald Francis, Acting Bowman Hugh Owen, Assistant Mechanic William M. Davies and Crew Members Hugh Jones, David Evans and Capt Jocelyn Jeavons for rescuing 10 crew from the Greek motor vessel *Nafsiporos* on 2 December 1966 during a hurricane. Holyhead's lifeboat crew also received awards.

1969 saw Coxswain Richard Evans received the British Empire Medal. He retired in 1970, and in sight of the lifeboat station he is commemorated with a 6ft bronze statue, unveiled on 23 November 2004 by Prince Charles. The magnificent statue was sculpted by Sam Holland whose grandfather had served on the Moelfre Lifeboat with Dic Evans. The statue cost £40,000 raised by an appeal and was helped in no small way by the local artist, the late Sir Kyffin Williams, who raised £20,000 from an arts sale.

Former Coxswain Richard Evans, BEM, who received two gold medals and one bronze medal, died on 13 September 2001.

The long standing tradition of life saving continues into the modern day and it was with great admiration that I was able to hear first-hand of the devotion to duty shown by the Moelfre lifeboat-men. Crew Member and Paramedic, David 'Dave' Massey described to me two particular rescue operations that had taken place, where honours were bestowed on crew members. The first he recalled was from July 1995.

At 3.47am on 1 July 1995, the *Robert and Violet* was launched, after a red flare had been sighted. Visibility was good with a strong ENE wind and choppy seas. Under the command of Coxswain Thomas Jones, the lifeboat quickly reached the casualty, which was a 30ft catamaran *Alleycat*, which had been caught on a lee-shore, meaning the wind is blowing towards it, and was trying to motor clear. On board were a man, and a woman who was totally exhausted. With less than 6ft of water beneath the keel of the lifeboat, Coxswain Jones felt that the catamaran was in imminent danger of being driven ashore and assistance was offered to the craft's owner, but initially was declined. Coxswain Jones then advised him to follow the lifeboat out into deeper water and this he attempted to do, but the craft then went into a very tight turn. It was only then realised that the catamaran had two anchors down, which were stopping any progress.

It was obvious that if the skipper left the helm to recover the anchors, the catamaran would very quickly lie beam-on to the breaking seas and could soon be ashore. The skipper then accepted the offer of help in recovering his anchors and he was instructed to keep the catamaran head-to-sea. Coxswain Jones took the lifeboat in towards the catamaran's starboard side, and as the two boats came together, lifeboat-man Rodney Pace got aboard but he found the craft's cockpit was badly cluttered with all sorts of gear, making boarding extremely difficult and the lifeboat-man got one leg into the cockpit, with his right leg trailing behind him, over the guard rails. As the lifeboat pulled clear, stern first, his right leg got caught between the belting on the lifeboat and the side deck of the catamaran. David Massey immediately volunteered to board the catamaran as being a paramedic could assist his injured colleague. Coxswain Jones brought the lifeboat back alongside the catamaran but further forward this time and David, with some first aid equipment got on board, but as he moved aft, along the very narrow side decking of the catamaran his lower leg was struck by the belting of the lifeboat as she pulled clear, astern. However, despite his own injuries, he managed to get to Rod Pace and administer first aid. Coxswain Jones then instructed the skipper to take a tow-line and, with Rod Pace, at the helm, the skipper moved forward, took the tow-line and recovered both anchors.

Coxswain Jones set course for Puffin Island and a helicopter was requested to take the two injured lifeboat-men off the catamaran. The 'Atlantic 21' class ILB from Beaumaris was launched, to take a doctor out and they met up with the Moelfre lifeboat at 6.06am, in the more sheltered waters off the south-west corner of Puffin Island, where Dr Hywel Jones was put on board the catamaran. There, together with one of the Beaumaris lifeboat-men, he assessed the situation and administered first-aid. Shortly afterwards the helicopter from RAF Valley arrived overhead and the two injured lifeboat-men were transferred to the Beaumaris ILB, from where they were airlifted-off and flown to hospital.

Rod Pace had sustained a fractured leg and Dave Massey had a fractured ankle. The Director of the RNLI later sent each of them a 'Letter of Thanks' 'for your gallant efforts while in pain and for your devotion to duty'.

At 12.35am on 17 June 2002, the *Robert and Violet* was launched, to the aid of the auxiliary-yacht *Annarchy*, with a crew of two which was in difficulties, nine miles north-west of Moelfre, in very rough seas, poor visibility, and a south-westerly gale, which was gusting up to storm-force 10, with wind speeds of over 60mph being recorded. While motor sailing from Liverpool to Beaumaris, the yacht's engine failed and the owner, having to row single handed was unable to make any progress to the south but was holding a course to the NNW. Once clear of the shelter of the land, the lifeboat was exposed to the full fury of the storm from astern, with waves up to 14ft high and with short, very steep seas. They came upon the casualty at 1.05am and found the yacht steering a very erratic course, with her jib and main-sail heavily reefed, but sheeted fully out. Coxswain Tony Barclay realised that, as the owner was in effect sailing single handed, a lifeboat-man would have to be put aboard the yacht and, because of his experience, maturity and sailing knowledge, it was agreed that Second Coxswain Rod Pace would be the best man for the job. Both he and the Coxswain Barclay were fully aware of the considerable risks involved in the planned move, in the pitch dark and violent seas.

The crew pose for the camera at the annual Moelfre Lifeboat day, an event that attracts thousands of visitors to the small village.

As the waves passed under the yacht, she was paying off by some 40° or more each time, making the approach of the lifeboat particularly difficult and Coxswain Barclay made five attempts to get close to the yacht, having to take evasive action several times, in order to avoid a collision. On the sixth attempt he was able to manoeuvre the lifeboat close enough for Rod Pace to jump across onto the yacht. For several moments, he clung onto the coach-house roof as the yacht rolled and pitched violently, before he was able to make his way aft, and into the cockpit. Once the jib had been furled and he had sheeted-in the boom, to regain control of the yacht, he signalled that he was ready to receive the tow-line. With no safety-line rigging on deck for him to clip onto, he carefully made his way forwards, as Coxswain Barclay skilfully manoeuvred the lifeboat close enough to the yacht's starboard bow, for a light heaving-line to be passed across at the first attempt, but as he was hauling in the line the yacht suddenly veered off to port. Quickly, he turned the heaving-line up on the cleats, while the crew of the lifeboat paid out the line as quickly as they could, Coxswain Barclay skilfully manoeuvring the lifeboat so as to retain contact with the yacht.

Once the tow-line had been hauled across and secured, Rod Pace returned to the comparative safety of the yacht's cockpit and he lowered the main-sail and secured it. At 1.45am, with Rod Pace at the helm of the yacht, the tow got under way, Coxswain Barclay being able to make about 4 knots, as he headed slowly back towards Moelfre, against the wind. No further problems were encountered and at 4am, the yacht was secured to the lifeboat's mooring-buoy near the boathouse.

For his outstanding courage in boarding the yacht and his subsequent excellent seamanship, the RNLI awarded its Thanks on Vellum to Second Coxswain Rodney Pace. For his excellent seamanship, courage and fine leadership, Coxswain Anthony Barclay was awarded a 'Framed letter of Thanks', signed by the Chairman of the RNLI. For their part in this excellent service, Vellum Service Certificates were presented to each of the other lifeboat-men involved, Deputy Second Coxswain David Williams, Third Mechanic David Jones, Emergency Mechanic Vincent Jones, and lifeboat-men David Peter Jones and Gary Roberts.

In 2002 at the age of 19 Vincent Jones was appointed motor mechanic becoming the youngest man ever to hold such a post in the RNLI.

The station's *Robert and Violet* is a Tyne class lifeboat, the first 'fast' slipway lifeboat, but it can also lie afloat. Features include a low-profile wheelhouse and a separate cabin behind the upper steering position. The propellers are protected by substantial bilge keels. The lifeboat is 47ft in length with a range of up to 240 nautical miles and facilitates a crew of six. The engines are 525hp with a speed of 18 knots equivalent to just over 20mph land speed. The last Tyne was built in 1990 and the class will be gradually replaced by the Tamar class.

The stations can also call upon their inshore D class boat that has been the workhorse of the service for 40 years. It is small and highly manoeuvrable, making it ideal for rescues close to shore, in fair to moderate conditions. It has a single outboard engine and can be righted manually by the crew following a capsize. The design of the D class has continued to evolve since its introduction.

Since 1848 conventional lifeboats at Moelfre have answered over 650 calls and saved over 750 lives, while the D class Inshore Lifeboat has answered over 800 calls and saved more the 650 lives. An exceptionally high standard of service has been established by generations of Moelfre lifeboat-men of which everyone in the area can be truly proud.

The RNLI is an independent charity, and does not receive any funding from the UK government. The volunteer lifeboat crews and lifeguards can't save lives at sea without your support.

Robert and Violet is soon to be replaced by the larger faster Tamar Class, a move that necessitates the rebuilding of the lifeboat station to accommodate the much larger vessel. During construction the lifeboat will lie afloat.

TRWYN DU LIGHTHOUSE

Trwyn Du Lighthouse is to be found on a magnificent stretch of coast line half a mile north-east from Penmon toll gate. The old Pilot houses, together with the old Lifeboat Station nearby, provides a true sense of tranquillity to the location. The lighthouse established in 1838 stands 95ft high, its light has a range of 12 nautical miles and is said to be the equivalent of 15,000 candelas with its white light flashing every five seconds. The lighthouse is painted in a distinctive black and white to aid daytime navigation around these treacherous waters between Anglesey and Puffin Island.

The lighthouse was manned by two keepers before automation in 1922. The light was converted to solar power in 1996 with a mechanism put in place to operate the 28 stone fog bell which rings out every 30 seconds to warn present day seafarers of the tidal dangers. The old lifeboat station pre dates the lighthouse built in 1832 and the crew were to serve the area admirably until 1915 when the station finally closed. During that time the lifeboat was called upon to attend over 50 rescue missions and it is reported to have saved the lives of 116 souls. The area around the eastern end of The Menai Strait was notorious for shipwrecks.

Trwyn Du Lighthouse was built following a major loss of life when a steamer ran aground near Puffin Island in 1831. On 17 August the steamer *Rothsay Castle* left Liverpool on a regular passage through the Menai Strait with 150 passengers aboard. The sea conditions were described as very difficult. Struggling against headwinds after an incredible 14 hours and now past midnight, she struck the Dutchman bank and with further collision along the channel she began to break up.

Trwyn Du Lighthouse built in 1838 was converted to solar power in 1996 with mechanism put in place to operate the 178kg or 28 stone fog bell which rings out every 30 seconds to warn present day seafarers of the tidal dangers.

The puffins from which the island takes its name, although known as Priestholm Ynys Seiriol in Welsh have shown an increase in breeding pairs in recent years following decimation on the island due to the accidental introduction of brown rats in the 19th century.

Despite the brave efforts of the Beaumaris lifeboat crew and the pilot from Penmon, only 20 of the passengers survived, with the loss of life reaching 130 that night. The captain and his officers were said to have been thrown overboard when the steamer's funnel broke off. Surviving passengers described afterwards that they had requested the captain turn back when they were only four hours out from Liverpool.

The *Rothsay Castle* was a paddle steamer originally built to carry passengers on the River Clyde between Invergary and Glasgow. The steamer was bought by a Liverpool businessman to run between Liverpool and Wexford taking it through the notorious waters at the northern entrance to the Menai Strait. There were reports that sailors had refused to work onboard as it was believed the vessel was not seaworthy. When the official report into the wrecking was made, it revealed several errors and cited that the ship was overcrowded. The steamer was said to have been leaking, with the holds submerged before the vessel reached the Great Orme. By the time it reached Puffin Island, the head of steam was so low that it was impossible to keep a course against the strong tide, with the result that it was said she had repeatedly grounded before finally breaking up.

As a consequence of the disaster, the lifeboat station was established at Penmon in 1831 and the subsequent building of the lighthouse was begun in 1835. The shipwreck was to become the centre of attention at the North Wales Eisteddfod held at Beaumaris in 1832, where Princess Victoria, later to become Queen Victoria, presented the winner of a poetry competition focused on the *Rothsay Castle* wrecking.

BEAUMARIS

Work began on Beaumaris Castle in 1295, on what was to be the last of the 'iron ring' of North Wales. However, unlike Caernarfon the castle was never finished, as money and supplies had run out before the castle was fully fortified. Edward I's last castle was built on a new site, allowing what has been described as an 'imaginative design creating possibly the most advanced mediaeval military architecture in Britain'. The castle has been dedicated as a World Heritage Site.

Designed by James of St George, the King's military architect, it was built to almost geometric symmetry with a high inner ring of defences surrounded by a circuit of walls, at ground level the defences were further strengthened, by the presence of a water filled moat, 18ft wide. A tidal dock was constructed at the southern end, allowing the largest vessels of the day to sail alongside.

Edward I had earlier designated the town of Llanfaes to be a seat of government when he visited in 1283. It was the defeat of the Welsh under Madog ap Llywelyn, also known as Prince Madoc, from the House of Aberffraw that led to Edward I demonstrating his power by actions we have already discovered at Newborough. Madog ap Llywelyn had put himself at the head of a national revolt in response to the actions of the royal administrators in North Wales. Following Edward I's victory he moved the entire population of Llanfaes to make way for his new castle.

Built as it was on former open marshland, the name Beaumaris was derived from the Norman-French beau, meaning fine or fair, and marais, meaning marshland, by the Normans who built the castle and town.

Building began at great speed, with upwards of 3,500 workmen employed at peak times of construction, and continued for 35 years. With the Welsh conquest almost concluded, finances and material ran out when Edward I turned his attentions towards Scotland, and the castle was never fully completed.

Seeing only limited action during the Civil War, the castle was, however, formidable. Any would be attacker would have to overcome as many as 14 separate defences, including strategically designed arrow slits within the castle walls, and murder holes, a hole through which the garrison could fire arrows, throw rocks, or pour harmful substances, such as scalding water and quicklime.

The town of Beaumaris nestles on the shores of the Menai Strait, famous not only for the castle but rich in architectural heritage. The town boasts a Victorian pier, a courthouse and gaol. The town courthouse was built in 1614, with the parish church of St Mary's, the town gaol and the Tudor Rose, one of the oldest timber-framed buildings in Britain, built during the 14th century. The lifeboat at Beaumaris is responsible for the waters of the Menai Strait between Anglesey and the North Wales coast. The RNLI station was presented with one of the first lifeboats originally provided by the Blue Peter television programme during 1967, as a result of the programme's 1966 lifeboat appeal.

Beaumaris Castle has been dedicated as a World Heritage Site.

At ground level the defences were further strengthened by the presence of a water filled moat, 18ft wide.

From Beaumaris the A545 hugs the coast for 4.5 miles back to Thomas Telford's suspension bridge. The majestic mountains of Snowdonia dominate the view across the Menai Strait, seeming almost within touching distance when sporting their winter coat. Our journey began in Porthmadog and has witnessed over 180 miles of some of the most beautiful, unspoilt, seaboard to be found anywhere in Britain, a landscape of immense beauty, with a history that dates back to Neolithic times.

Home to the Ffestiniog Railway, founded by an Act of Parliament in 1832 and now the oldest railway company in the world still running trains was our introduction to the Lleyn Peninsula. A detour to the inspirational Italianate village of Portmeirion followed, before heading west along the southern shores of Llŷn, benefiting as it does from the Gulf Stream. We discovered the impressive castle at Criccieth, dominating the town. Pwllheli, the unofficial capital of Llŷn before taking in the delightful seaside villages of LLanbedrog, Abersoch and Aberdaron.

Tales of shipwrecks and smuggling and quiet sandy coves all abound on the more rugged, northern shores of Llŷn. Nestling in the most serene and picturesque settings we visited some of Llŷn's delightful churches, most set within sight of the sea, and important stopping off points for pilgrims, on their journey to Bardsey Island. Rising abruptly from the sea and towering over the original site of the cursed village of Nant Gwrtheyrn was the summit of Llŷn, Yr Eifl, where we stood over 1,800ft above the sea, rewarded with the most awe-inspiring views afforded anywhere in Britain. With Anglesey in sight we came to Caernarfon Castle, Edward I's seat of dominance, guarding as it does the entrance to the Menai Strait, before crossing to Anglesey by means of Thomas Telford's magnificent suspension bridge.

The relatively flat tidal estuaries of Anglesey's west coast were explored, where we visted the extensive sand dunes of Newborough Warren, before visiting St Cwyfan's Church, often referred to as the church in the sea. The modern day is represented at RAF Valley, ahead of Holy Island and the lighthouse at South Stack. The journey then continued to Anglesey's east coast, with a visit to Llynnon Mill, at the heart of the island en route.

The tragic tale of the the *Royal Charter* and an ancient burial chamber said to date from 2000BC were discovered at Moelfre where the renowned lifeboat station's crews gallantry was revealed before reaching Penmon, concluding at Beaumaris. The journey of discovery has been a delight to take and I hope the book will encourage you to visit, as you can be assured of a warm welcome. Visit during the summer when the weather can provide you with balmy summer days, or come during winter when wild stormy days and tranquil frosty ones will provide you with inspiration.

Thank you for joining me on this wonderful journey of discovery.

Snowdon 'Yr Wyddfa' from Yr Eifl, the summit of the Lleyn Peninsula. The mountain mass of Snowdonia dominates the distant views of both Llŷn and Anglesey providing a magnificent backdrop.